ITALIAN LANDSCAPE POEMS

Also by Alistair Elliot

POETRY

Contentions (Ceolfrith Press, 1977)
Kisses (Ceolfrith Press, 1977)
Talking to Bede (MidNAG, 1982)
Talking Back (Secker & Warburg, 1982)
On the Appian Way (Secker & Warburg, 1984)
My Country: Collected Poems (Carcanet, 1989)
Turning the Stones (Carcanet, 1993)

TRANSLATIONS

Euripides: *Alcestis* (Chandler, San Francisco, 1965)
Aristophanes: *Peace*, in *Greek Comedy* (Dell, New York, 1965)
Paul Verlaine: *Femmes/Hombres* (Anvil Press, 1979;
    Sheep Meadow Press, New York, 1984)
Heinrich Heine: *The Lazarus Poems* (MidNAG/Carcanet, 1979)
French Love Poems (Bloodaxe Books, 1991)
Euripides: *Medea* (performed Almeida Theatre, 1992;
    published Oberon Books, 1993)

EDITOR

Virgil: The Georgics, with John Dryden's Translation
    (MidNAG, 1981)

Italian Landscape Poems

TRANSLATED BY
Alistair Elliot

BLOODAXE BOOKS

ISBN: 1 85224 247 7

First published 1993 by
Bloodaxe Books Ltd,
P.O. Box 1SN,
Newcastle upon Tyne NE99 1SN.

Bloodaxe Books Ltd acknowledges
the financial assistance of Northern Arts.

ACKNOWLEDGEMENTS

Alistair Elliot acknowledges a grant from the Arts Council
for travel in Italy, partly related to this book,
partly to other literary projects.
Thanks are also due to Hugh Shankland
for his valuable advice.

Cover printing by J. Thomson Colour Printers Ltd, Glasgow.

Printed in Great Britain by
Bell & Bain Limited, Glasgow, Scotland.

CONTENTS

PREFACE

This book was to be like my *French Love Poems*, chosen and translated by me, only Italian and about the *paese*. By this I didn't mean the national paese, Italy itself – I didn't want to rake together a lot of patriotic odes (always skipped in anthologies); but the other meaning of paese seemed very promising: 'my town, my village, the countryside I come from' is somehow a characteristic strand in Italian life. However, again, my enthusiasm received a check: as I began searching I foresaw that there was a danger of looking for poems about particular places to fill gaps, like a social investigator trying to keep the survey balanced. I would wind up including some doughy verse because I hadn't covered the Abruzzi properly, or needed something medieval about Naples, or the other Greek cities of the south.

Giving the book a title helped me escape from this restriction: *Italian Poems of Place* sounds unattractive. But with *Italian Landscape Poems* I saw that, stretching a point, I could include St Francis' famous vision of the elements as part of our family, as well as clear pictures of actual views like Saba's 'Ulisse' and D'Annunzio's 'I pastori'. I could include odd angles like Dante's use of landscape as punishment and Ariosto's wry sexscapes (the literary equivalent of Arcimboldo's vegetable portraits). The countryside as a place to stimulate thought (Leopardi) or terror (Belli) was also a place for visions (D'Annunzio's 'Bocca d'Arno') and nostalgia (Pascoli).

As I worked through the centuries and the famous names, another theme appeared: the history of taste in views – the "horrid" (what makes your hair stand on end) becoming the "picturesque" (what is paintable), just as in verse the banal comic detail ('men in shirt-sleeves') can become touching and "poetic" in a later age. The historical ignoramus imagines changes like that go in a simple curve, so it is refreshing to see that Dante's sense of a landscape is as actual as Saba's and that an intelligent writer can step off that curving line onto another which has never led anywhere – I think of Lorenzo de' Medici, so educated, declaring like a peasant that a certain valley in Tuscany is the most beautiful in the world because Nature made it just right for falconers, and giving us a poem that might have been written by a journalist as good as Hazlitt.

Thus my samples of Italian poetry jostle and contradict each other. So much the better – there are plenty of other voices that could add their say. Indeed, I would have liked to embrace many more, including more of our contemporaries, but one can meet too many poets at once, and this is meant to be an introduction.

ITALIAN LANDSCAPE POEMS

Laudes creaturarum

Altissimu, onnipotente, bon Signore,
tue so' le laude, la gloria e l'honore et onne benedictione.
Ad te solo, Altissimo, se konfano,
et nullu homo ene dignu te mentovare.

Laudato sie, mi Signore, cum tucte le tue creature:
spetialmente messor lo frate Sole,
lo qual è jorno, et allumini noi per loi;
et ellu è bellu e radiante, cum grande splendore;
de te, Altissimo, porta significatione.

Laudato si', mi Signore, per sora Luna e le Stelle,
in celu l'ài formate clarite et pretiose et belle.

Laudato si', mi Signore, per frate Vento,
et per Aere et Nubilo et Sereno et onne Tempo,
per lo quale a le tue creature dai sustentamento.

Laudato si', mi Signore, per sor'Aqua,
la quale è multo utile et humile et pretiosa et casta.

Laudato si', mi Signore, per frate Focu,
per lo quale ennallumini la nocte,
ed ello è bello et jocundo et robustoso et forte.

Laudato si', mi Signore, per sora nostra matre Terra,
la quale ne sustenta et governa
et produce diversi fructi con coloriti flori et herba.

Laudato si', mi Signore, per quelli ke perdonano per lo tuo amore
et sostengo infirmitate et tribulatione;
beati quelli ke 'l sosterrano in pace,
ka da te, Altissimo, sirano incoronati.

Psalm of the Creatures

O highest Lord, all-powerful and good,
yours are the praise, the glory and the honour and every word
of blessing.
To you alone, O Highest, they belong:
and no man is good enough to name your Name.

May you be praised, my Lord, with all your creatures,
and specially master brother Sun,
who is the day and you give us light through him,
and he is lovely and radiant with great splendour:
O Highest, he bears your sign, he stands for you.

May you be praised, my Lord, through sister Moon and the Stars:
in heaven you shaped them, shining and precious and lovely.

May you be praised, my Lord, through brother Wind
and through Air and Clouds, Fair Sky, and every Weather,
through all of whom you bring nourishment to your creatures.

May you be praised, my Lord, through sister Water,
who is so helpful and humble, precious and chaste.

May you be praised, my Lord, through brother Fire,
by whom you give us light in the darkness
and he is lovely and playful, and sturdy and strong.

May you be praised, my Lord, through our sister mother Earth,
who nourishes and guides us
and brings forth fruit in kinds, with coloured flowers, and grass.

May you be praised, my Lord, through those who bring forgiveness
through your love
and bear infirmity and tribulation.
Blessed be those who endure these things in peace
for from you, O Highest, they shall receive a crown.

Laudato si', mi Signore, per sora nostra Morte corporale,
da la quale nullu homo vivente pò skappare:
guai a cquelli ke morrano ne le peccata mortali;
beati quelli ke trovarà ne le tue sanctissime voluntati,
ka la morte secunda nol farrà male.

Laudate et benedicete mi Signore et rengratiate.
et serviateli cum grande humilitate.

SAN FRANCESCO D'ASSISI
(*c*.1182-1226)

May you be praised, my Lord, through our sister bodily Death
from whom no man alive can ever escape.
Woe to those who will die in the midst of mortal sins.
Blessed be those she finds performing your holy will;
for the second death will not be harming them.

Praise and bless my Lord and give him thanks,
and be his servants as humbly as we can.

SAINT FRANCIS OF ASSISI

Inferno, Canto XXX, 49-75

Io vidi un, fatto a guisa di lëuto,
  pur ch'elli avesse avuta l'anguinaia
  tronca da l'altro che l'uomo ha forcuto.

La grave idropesì, che sì dispaia
  le membra con l'omor che mal converte,
  che 'l viso non risponde a la ventraia,

faceva lui tener le labbra aperte
  come l'etico fa, che per la sete
  l'un verso 'l mento e l'altro in sù rinverte.

'O voi che sanz' alcuna pena siete,
  e non so io perché, nel mondo gramo,'
  diss' elli a noi, 'guardate e attendete

a la miseria del maestro Adamo;
  io ebbi, vivo, assai di quel ch'i' volli,
  e ora, lasso!, un gocciol d'acqua bramo.

Li ruscelletti che d'i verdi colli
  del Casentin discendon giuso in Arno,
  faccendo i lor canali freddi e molli,

sempre mi stanno innanzi, e non indarno,
  ché l'imagine lor vie più m'asciuga
  che 'l male ond' io nel volto mi discarno.

La rigida giustizia che mi fruga
  tragge cagion del loco ov' io peccai
  a metter più li miei sospiri in fuga.

Ivi è Romena, là dov' io falsai
  la lega suggellata del Batista;
  per ch'io il corpo sù arso lasciai.

DANTE ALIGHIERI
(1265-1321)

An Englishman in Hell

I saw one shaped as if he were a lute –
if he had had the parts below the groin
cut off, where man is forked and grows a shoot.

A heavy dropsy so unequally
filled out his limbs with undigested fluid
it made his face no longer match his belly:

also it made him hold his lips wide open
as fever-patients do, who in their thirst
curl one lip upward, one towards the chin.

'O you who come,' he said, 'I don't know how,
without a punishment to the world of pain,
look, both of you, on Master Adam now

and contemplate my misery while you stop:
alive, I had my fill of all I wanted,
now all I want is a single water-drop.

The little brooks which down from the green hills
of Casentino splash towards the Arno,
making their channels smooth and soft and chill,

hang always here before me – not in vain:
for the image of them desiccates me more
than this disease, which sucks my face so thin.

Unbending Justice, searching through my life,
found in the place where I once sinned a sight
to make me sigh the faster for relief.

For among them is Romena, where I turned
the false alloy to coins with St John's head:
for which, I left my body up there, burned...'

DANTE ALIGHIERI
from *The Divine Comedy*

Canzone CLXIV

Or che 'l ciel e la terra e 'l vento tace,
e le fere e gli augelli il sonno affrena,
notte il carro stellato in giro mena
e nel suo letto il mar senz'onda giace;

vegghio, penso, ardo, piango, e chi mi sface
sempre m'è inanzi per mia dolce pena;
guerra è 'l mio stato, d'ira e di duol piena,
e sol di lei pensando ò qualche pace.

Così sol d'una chiara fonte viva
move 'l dolce e l'amaro ond'io mi pasco;
una man sola mi risana e punge;

e perché 'l mio martir non giunga a riva,
mille volte il dì moro e mille nasco:
tanto da la salute mia son lunge!

FRANCESCO PETRARCA
(1304-74)

14

Sonnet 164

Now sky's at peace with earth, and winds disarm,
And sleep hobbles the beasts and birds, and night
Leads round its carriage pricked with starry light,
And in its seamless bed the sea lies calm;

But I wake, think, burn, weep; and always find
She who destroys me, there, to my sweet pain:
My state of war, where rage and grief remain,
And only thoughts of her can soothe my mind.

So from one single clear and lively spring
The sweet and bitter that I live on flow:
The same hand heals me that has dealt the blow.

And, not to reach an end to suffering,
I die, I'm born, a thousand times a day,
For my salvation lies so far away.

FRANCESCO PETRARCA

Canzone CCXIX

Il cantar novo e 'l pianger delli augelli
in sul dì fanno retentir le valli,
e 'l mormorar de' liquidi cristalli
giù per lucidi freschi rivi e snelli.

Quella ch'à neve il volto, oro i capelli,
nel cui amor non fur mai inganni né falli,
destami al suon delli amorosi balli,
pettinando al suo vecchio i bianchi velli.

Così mi sveglio a salutar l'aurora
e 'l sol ch'è seco, e più l'altro ond'io fui
ne' primi anni abbagliato e son ancora;

i' gli ò veduti alcun giorno ambedui
levarsi inseme, e 'n un punto e 'n un'ora
quel far le stelle, e questo sparir lui.

FRANCESCO PETRARCA

Sonnet 219

The morning songs of birds on their sad themes
at daybreak fill the dene with echoing calls,
and there's the sigh as liquid crystals fall,
pouring in brisk and chilly shining streams.

She who has snow for cheeks, gold on her head,
whose love has no deceit, no sidelong glances,
stirs me from sleep with this sound of amorous dances,
combing her old man's bristles, still in bed.

So I wake up to greet the dawn; the sun
that's with her; and that sun which struck my eyes
when I was young and has dazzled me since then.

One day I saw them both stretch up a limb
from their horizons and together rise:
he made the stars invisible, and she him.

FRANCESCO PETRARCA

Ballata

O vaghe montanine pasturelle,
d'onde venite sì leggiadre e belle?

Qual'è il paese dove nate sète,
che sì bel frutto più che gli altri adduce?
Creature d'Amor voi mi parete,
tanto la vostra vista adorna luce!
Nè oro nè argento in voi riluce,
e, mal vestite, parete angiolelle.

'Noi stiamo in alpe presso ad un boschetto;
povera capannetta è 'l nostro sito:
col padre e con la madre in picciol letto,
torniam la sera dal prato fiorito,
dove natura ci ha sempre nodrito,
guardando il dì le nostre pecorelle.'

'Assai si dee doler vostra bellezza,
quando tra monti e valle la mostrate;
chè non è terra di sì grande altezza,
dove non foste degne ed onorate.
Deh, ditemi se voi vi contentate
di star nei boschi così poverelle.'

'Più si contenta ciascuna di noi
andar dietro alle mandre alla pastura,
che non farebbe qual fosse di voi
d'andare a festa dentro vostre mura.
Ricchezze non cerchiam, nè più ventura,
che balli, canti e fiori e ghirlandelle.'

Ballata, s'io fossi come già fui,
diventerei pastore e montanino;
e prima che io il dicessi altrui,
sarei al loco di costor vicino;
ed or direi, 'Biondella', ed or 'Martino',
seguendo sempre dove andasser elle.

FRANCO SACCHETTI
(c.1332-c.1400)

18

Shepherdesses

— Oh, mountain shepherdesses, young and fair!
Where do you come from with that charming air?

What's the *paese* you were born into,
Which bears such fruit, finer than other places?
I think that Love must have created you —
Such light comes beaming from your pretty faces!
No gold or silver gleams upon your dresses:
You look like angels in robes that need repair.

— We live on the high fell beside a wood.
There's a poor hut, a shanty but it's ours,
With Father and Mother sharing our little bed.
We watch the sheep all day, till the sun lowers,
Then we go home from pastures full of flowers:
Nature has given us all we needed there.

— Surely your beauty has complaints of fate?
Shown among cliffs, in eyeless country pent...
There is no city in the world so great
You'd not be welcome, and an ornament.
Come, tell me, will you really stay, content,
So poor and humble in your wooded lair?

— Oh, we are happier, we all agree,
Going to pasture following the beasts
Than we imagine you can ever be
Inside your walls at parties and at feasts.
We don't want wealth or grand events — we're pleased
With songs and dances, with flowers for our hair.

Oh ballad, if I were as I was once,
I'd run away to the hills and mind a flock:
Before I told my family or my friends,
I'd join the shepherd girls and take a rock
Near theirs; call out to 'Charlie' and 'White Sock';
And follow where they led me, everywhere.

FRANCO SACCHETTI

Uccellagione di starne

Era già rosso tutto l'oriente
e le cime de' monti parien d'oro:
la passeretta schiamazzar si sente,
e 'l contadin tornava al suo lavoro:
le stelle eran fuggite, e già presente
si vedea quasi quel ch'amò l'alloro.
Ritornavansi al bosco molto in fretta
l'allocco, il barbagianni e la civetta.

La volpe ritornava alla sua tana
e 'l lupo ritornava al suo deserto;
era venuta e sparita Diana,
però forse saria suto scoperto.
Avea già la sollecita villana
alle pecore e' porci l'uscio aperto.
Netta era l'aria, fresca e cristallina,
e da sperar buon tempo la mattina,

quando io fu' desto da certi romori
di buon sonagli ed allettar di cani:
– Or su andianne presto, uccellatori,
perché gli è tardi e i luoghi son lontani:
el canattier sia 'l primo ch'esca fuori,
acciò che i piè de' cavalli stamani
non ci guastassin di can qualche paio:
deh! vanne presto innanzi, Cappellaio –.

Adunque il Cappellaio innanzi cammina:
chiama Tamburo e Pezzuolo e Martello,
la Foglia e la Castagna e la Guerrina,
Fagiano e Fagianin, Rocca e Cappello,
e Frizza e Biondo, Bamboccio e Rosina;
Ghiotto, la Corta, Viola e Pestello,
e Serchio e Fuso e 'l mio Buontempo vecchio,
Zambraccio, Buratel, Staccio e Pennecchio.

Hawking for Partridges

It was already pink across the east
and every hill-top had a golden look;
the labourer was returning from his rest,
and the young sparrows had begun to squeak;
the stars had fled; and now, the one who chased
the laurel, loomed on the skyline, coming back.
Now home in haste to ruins, trees and holes
floated the tawny, barn and little owls.

The fox was trotting sidelong to his den,
the wolf retreating to his wilderness
(Apollo's sister having shone and gone),
shy of discovery in the brighter rays.
The early peasant girls came out to open
gates for their sheep and pigs to root and graze.
The air was limpid, cool and crystalline,
a morning to imply it would stay fine,

when I was wakened up by the familiar
noises of falcon bells, soft talk to hounds:
'Get up, come on, we've got to go, you fowlers;
it's getting late, the place is quite a distance;
the first to leave must be the dogs and handler:
today we don't want any incidents
of dogs being damaged by some heavy hoof.
Lead out then, Cappellaio, sharpish, move!'

So Cappellaio takes them off in front,
calling their names out: Drum and Rag and Hammer,
Leafy and Chestnut Girl and Little Fighter,
Pheasant and Pheasantino, Distaff, Hoody,
Fizzy and Blondo, Dopey Kid and Pinky,
Greedy, then Shorty, Violet and the Pestle,
Splasher and Spindle, good old Goodtimes too,
Dirty, the Sifter, and the Sieve, and Plume.

Quando hanno i can di campo preso un pezzo,
quattro seguivan con quattro sparvieri:
Guglielmo, che per suo antico vezzo
sempre quest'arte ha fatto volentieri;
Giovan Francesco, e Dionigi il sezzo,
ché innanzi a lui cavalca el Foglia Amieri;
ma, perché era buon'ora la mattina,
mentre cavalca Dionigi inchina.

Ma la Fortuna, che ha sempre piacere
di far diventar brun quel ch'è più bianco,
dormendo Dionigi fe' cadere
appunto per disgrazia al lato manco;
sì che cadendo addosso allo sparviere,
ruppeli un'alia e macerolli il fianco:
questo gli piacque assai, benché io nol dica,
ché gli par esser fuor di gran fatica.

Non cadde Dionigi, ma rovina,
e, come debbi creder, toccò fondo;
ché, com'un tratto egli ha preso la china,
presto la truova com'un sasso tondo.
Disse fra sé: – Meglio era stamattina
restar nel letto, come fe' Gismondo,
scalzo e in camicia sulle pocce al fresco:
non c'inciampo mai più, se di questa esco.

Io ho avuto pur poco intelletto
ad uscire staman sì tosto fuori:
se mi restavo in casa nel mio letto,
per me meglio era, e per gli uccellatori;
messo arei il disinar bene in assetto,
e la tovaglia adorna di bei fiori.
Meglio è straccar la coltrice e 'l guanciale
che 'l cavallo e 'l famiglio e farsi male –.

Intanto vuol lo sparviere impugnare,
ma gli è sì rotto che non può far l'erta;
Dionigi con la man l'usa aiutare,
e pur ricade, e di questo s'accerta
che d'altro gli bisogna procacciare;
nel rassettargli la manica aperta
le man ghermigli; e lui sotto sel caccia,
saltogli addosso, e fenne una cofaccia.

When all these dogs had gone some space ahead,
four riders followed, holding each a hawk:
Guglielmo, mad about this art and glad
to practise ever since he learned the knack;
Giovan Francesco; and last Dionigi, padding
behind, at Foglia Amieri's bobbing back –
though it was still so early that he made
deeper and deeper bows to his horse's head.

But Lady Fortune, who delights to call
a bit of darkness down on days too bright,
made Dionigi fall asleep and fall
(of course) by accident on his sinister side;
so that he dropped down right on top of the falcon,
and broke its wing and crushed its leg and side.
This pleased him greatly (someone else might say):
it let him off the labours of the day.

Dionigi didn't so much fall as stoop,
and must have hit at the bottom of his dive –
for when he once got moving down the slope
he rushed, like a round stone, at the objective.
Under his breath he said, 'I wish I'd stopped
in bed, like Sigismondo, and just skived
in comfort and shirt-tail, barefoot, on my tits:
this is the last time I trip up like this.

'Besides, it really was a little stupid
to get up and go out at such an hour:
if only I had stayed at home in bed...
Better for me, and for the other fowlers.
I would have seen to dinner being ready
in order, with an arrangement of nice flowers.
Better to wear your bedding to rags and dirt
than wear out horse and servant – and get hurt.'

He's trying to get the falcon on his fist
meanwhile, but it's so damaged it can't hop.
He helps it, nudging with the back of his wrist;
still it falls off again; he'll have to stop
dreaming and get another – this one's finished.
As he adjusts the glove, which had come open,
it claws his hands – he throws the creature down
and stamps, and leaves it flatter than a bun.

– Dov'è 'l Corona? Ov'è Giovan Simone? –
domanda' Braccio – ov'è quel del gran naso? –
Braccio rispose a me: – Varie cagione
fatto ha ch'ognun di loro si è rimaso.
Non prese mai il Corona uno starnone,
se per disgrazia non l'ha preso a caso:
se s'è lasciato adunque, non s'ingiuria;
menarlo seco è cattiva auguria –.

– Luigi Pulci ov'è, che non si sente? –
– Ei se n'andò là dianzi in quel boschetto,
ché qualche fantasia ha per la mente:
vorrà fantasticar forse un sonetto;
guarti, Corona, che, se non si pente,
e' borbottò staman molto nel letto,
e sentii ricordarli te, Corona,
e t'ha a cacciare in frottola o in canzona.

Giovan Simone ha già preso la piega
d'andarne sanza dire agli altri addio;
sanza licenzia n'è ito a bottega,
di che gran sete tiene e gran disio.
Luigi, quando il fiero naso piega,
cani e cavagli adombra e fa restio;
per questo ognun che resti si contenta;
ciò che lo vede fugge e si spaventa –.

Restono adunque tre da uccellare,
e drieto a questi andava molta gente;
chi per piacere e chi pur per guardare,
Bartolo ed Ulivier, Braccio e il Parente,
che mai non vide più starne volare;
ed io con lor mi missi; parimente
Pietro Alamanni e il Portinar Giovanni,
che pare in sulla nona un barbagianni.

Strozzo drieto a costor, come maestro
di questa gente, andava scosto un poco;
come quello che v'era molto destro
e molte volte ha fatto simil giuoco.
E tanto calvalcammo pel silvestro,
che finalmente fummo giunti al loco
più bel che mai vedessi creatura:
per uccellar l'ha fatto la natura.

'So where's Corona? Where's Giovan Simone?'
I asked, 'and where's our hero with The Nose?'
Braccio replied, 'It happens every one of
those three has stayed behind, for his own purpose.
Corona, your falconer, never yet brought down a
partridge – except by accident, God knows.
Bringing him brings bad luck. So he won't mind
our going out and leaving him behind.'

'Where's Pulci? I've not heard a word from him.'
'He's taken off into that wood ahead;
his mind is full of some poetic whim.
Perhaps he's got a sonnet in his head.
Watch it, Corona, he was mumbling rhymes
and syllables this morning in his bed:
your name is on it: if he doesn't change
his mind, you'll face a clerihew at close range.

'Giovan Simone has lately got the habit
of bolting off: he doesn't say goodbye
or by your leave, just vanishes like a rabbit
into a tavern, longing for it, dry.
When Pulci wrinkles his fierce nose, the shadow
startles the dogs and horses, and they shy;
if he's staying back, we hear it with delight:
things panic and run off when he's in sight.'

So now we're left with three hawks and three men,
and quite a lot of people riding after,
to join our pleasure or just see what happens,
Bartolo, Oliver, Braccio and my Father,
who never saw a partridge fly again;
I joined myself to this group; also there were
Alamanni (Peter) and Portinari (John) –
who looked just like an owl caught out at noon.

Fittingly, as the master of all these,
Strozzo came last, a little off the pace,
apart, like one who had the expertise
and knew the game from many similar days.
On we all rode our horses through the trees
until we reached at last the prettiest place
seen in this world by any human creature,
just made for hawking by the hand of nature:

E' si vedea una gentil valletta,
un fossatel con certe macchie in mezzo,
da ogni parte rimunita e netta;
sol nel fossato star possono a rezzo:
era da ogni lato una piaggetta,
che d'uccellar facea venir ribrezzo
a chi non avessi occhi, tanto è bella:
il mondo non ha una pari a quella.

Scaldava el sole al monte già le spalle,
e 'l resto della valle è ancora ombrosa,
quando, giunta la gente in su quel calle,
prima a vedere e disegnar si posa,
e poi si spargon tutti per la valle;
e perché a punto riesca ogni cosa,
chi va co' can, chi alla guardia, a getto,
sì come Strozzo ha ordinato e detto.

Era da ogni parte uno sparviere
alto in buon luogo da poter gittare;
l'altro a capo ne va del canattiere
e alla brigata lo vorrà scagliare;
era Bartolo al fondo ed Uliviere
ed alcun altro per poter guardare;
a mezza piaggia e in una bella stoppia,
il Cappellaio ai can leva la coppia.

Non altrimenti quando la trombetta
sente alle mosse il lieve barberesco,
parte correndo, o, vuo' dir, vola in fretta;
così quei can, che sciolti son di fresco:
e se non pur che 'l canattier gli alletta,
chiamando alcuni, ed a chi scuote il pesco,
sarebbe il seguitarli troppa pena:
pur la pertica e il fischio li raffrena.

– Tira, buon can, su; tira su, cammina;
andianne, andianne; torna qui, te', torna:
ah! sciagurato; Tamburo e Guerrina,
abbiate cura a Sacco che soggiorna;
ah! bugiardo, ah! poltron; volgi, Rosina:
guata, buon can, guata brigata adorna!
te', Fagiano; oh che volta fu mai quella! –
in questo modo il canattier favella.

A noble little valley, with a stream
and bushes here and there about the middle,
otherwise clear of thickets, and mown clean.
The stream-bed is the one place to keep cool,
with on each side a little bank of green
so lovely that the world can't parallel
its beauty, and even those who have no eye
for hawking, tremble with desire to try.

The sun was warming the shoulders of the hill,
though down the slope some shadow still remains,
when we arrived there on this path, and all
paused to look round and make some hunting plans,
and then dispersed ourselves about the dale:
and to be sure we do not waste our pains,
some take the hounds, some watch for game, some hand
the hawks, disposed by Strozzo's quiet command.

On either side and up a height one hawk
was stationed, in a good place to let fly.
The third, beside the handler of the pack,
advances, to be launched against the covey.
Bartolo stands near Oliver at the back
of the valley, with some others keeping cave.
Half up the slope, in a fair field of stubble,
Cappellaio stoops and frees his dogs from the couple.

It's like what happens when the barbary horse
hears the horn sound the signal for its race:
straight off it gallops (you want to say it flies) –
so do those dogs when they first feel release;
and now the kennelman must cajole and tease
and call and even knock them like fruit-trees;
or keeping up with them would be too much hassle:
he checks them, though, with rod and word and whistle.

'Keep it up; good dog; go on, keep it coming;
Let's move it, move it; hold on, here, come back;
Oh you poor mutt! Hey Fighter, you and Drum,
attend to Baggy, pointing, on the track –
You lying dog, you lazy...Turn your bum,
Pinky, this way! – look, look, my bonny pack! –
Oh, Pheasant, not up there! That must be wrong.'
Such is the kennelman's professional song.

– State avveduti. Ah! Staccio, frulla, frulla:
e che leva cacciando l'amor mio?
ma io non veggo però levar nulla,
e' n'ha pur voglia e n'ha pur gran disio.
Guarda la Corta là che si trastulla.
Oh che romor faranno! e già 'l sent'io.
Chi salta e balla e chi la leverà
di questi cani il miglior can serà.

Io veggo che Buontempo è in sulla traccia:
ve' che la corre e la farà levare:
abbi cura a Buontempo, ché la caccia;
parmi vederla e sentirla frullare:
benché e' sia vecchio assai, non ti dispiaccia;
ch'io l'ho veduto e so quel che sa fare;
io so che 'l mio Buontempo mai non erra.
Ecco: a te, Ulivier: guardala a terra.

Guarda quell'altra all'erta, una al fossato:
non ti diss'io che mi parea sentille?
guardane una alla vigna e l'altra a lato,
guardane dua da me, guardane mille –.
Alla brigata prima avea gittato
Giovan Francesco, ed empieva le ville
di grida e di conforti al suo uccello:
ma per la fretta gittò col cappello.

– Ecco, Guglielmo, a te una ne viene:
cava il cappello, ed alzerai la mano;
non istar più, Guglielmo; ecco, a te; bene –.
Guglielmo getta e grida: – Ahi! villano –.
Segue la starna, e drieto ben le tiene,
quello sparviere e in tempo momentano
dette in aria forse cento braccia;
poi cadde in terra, e già la pela e straccia.

– Garri a quel can – Guglielmo grida forte –
che corre per cavargliene di piè –.
E però che le pertiche eran corte,
un sasso prese ed a Guerrina die':
poi corre giù, sanz'aspettar più scorte;
e quando presso allo sparvier più è,
nollo veggendo, cheto usava stare,
per udir se lo sente sonagliare.

'Alert, now. Sieve, boy, hear them fluttering there?
And who's my love? Who's going to flush them out?
Come on boy, you've put nothing in the air –
I know he wants to, oh he wants the lot.
Shorty's just playing! Take a look at her!
What music they will make! I think I hear it!
You jump and dance about – but you must raise
one of them from the bushes to get praise.

'I see that Goodtimes there has found the scent –
See how he's running them, he'll start the flight –
All keep an eye on Goodtimes, he can hunt –
I think he sees them, and can hear them flutter.
He's old, he's very old, but never mind –
I've seen him work – he knows what he's about.
I know my Goodtimes and he doesn't flounder.
Look: there's one by you, Oliver, on the ground.

'There's one – on the steep bit; and one by the river bed.
Didn't I tell you I could hear the things?
And one among the vines, and one to the side;
Look, two right here by me; a thousand wings!'
Giovan Francesco was filling the countryside
meanwhile, with shouts of courage and strange urgings.
It seemed he'd launched his bird, and that was good:
but in the rush he'd not removed its hood.

'Look out, Guglielmo, one of them's coming at you:
Take off the hood, and lift her higher – stretch!
No need to hold back now – she's all yours – catch her.'
In one, Guglielmo launches and shouts 'Wretch!' –
The falcon chases fast and firmly lodges
his talons in the hind parts of the partridge
and they fly on perhaps a hundred beats,
then fall: the hawk already skins and eats.

'Growl at that dog,' Guglielmo shouted loud,
'to get me that bird out from underfoot.'
And as their rods and whips were all too short,
he pitched a stone at Fighter: 'Get them out;'
runs down himself, not waiting to be taught,
and though he cannot see it, when he's got
near where the hawk must be, he stands stock still
hoping to hear the falcon shake its bell.

E così stando, gliel venne veduto:
– Presto, – grida – a cavallo: e' l'ha pur presa –.
Lieto a lui vanne destro ed avveduto,
come colui che l'arte ha bene intesa;
preseli il geto e per quel l'ha tenuto;
dàlli il capo, e 'l cervel che non li pesa;
sghermillo, e l'unghia e 'l becco gli avea netto;
poi rimisse il cappello e torna a getto.

Giovan Francesco intanto avea ripreso
el suo sparviere e preso miglior loco;
parli veder che a lui ne venga teso
uno starnone: e come presso un poco
gli fu, egli ha tutte le dita steso
e gittò come mastro di tal gioco:
giunse la starna; e perché era la vecchia,
si fe' lasciare, e tutto lo spennecchia.

In vero egli era un certo sparverugio
che somigliava un gheppio, tanto è poco;
non credo preso avesse un calderugio:
se non faceva tosto, o in breve loco,
non avere' speranza nello indugio:
quando non piglia, e' si levava a gioco;
e la cagion che quel tratto non prese,
fu che non vi avea il capo e non vi attese.

Intanto venne uno starnone all'erta:
videlo il Foglia e fece un gentil getto:
lo sparvier vola per la piaggia aperta,
e présegliene innanzi al dirimpetto:
corre giù il Foglia, e pargliene aver certa,
però che lo sparvier molto è perfetto:
preselo al netto, ove non era stecco,
e in terra insanguinò li piedi e 'l becco:

e questo fe', ché lo sparviere è soro.
Ed intanto Ulivier forte gridava:
– Chiama giù il Cappellaio, chiama costoro.
Guardate; una n'è qua – così parlava –.
Tu lega i can, però che basta loro
la Rocca, che di sotterra le cava.
Vien giù, Guglielmo, non ti stare a rezzo:
e tu e 'l Foglia la mettete in mezzo –.

And standing there, he suddenly spots the birds:
'Here, quick,' he cries, 'we're off – the hound has caught it.'
It gladly comes to him, skilful and alert,
seeming to understand the art as he did.
He takes the jess and holds the hawk by that,
gives it the head and brain (he doesn't want it),
makes it relax its claws, cleans beak and talon,
and takes it back for launching, with its hood on.

Giovan Francesco meantime had recovered
his hawk and found a better place to stand.
Glimpsing a partridge gliding straight toward
his station, he extends his arm and hand
as it comes close, spreading his fingers wide,
and launches like a master in command:
it overtakes but lets the prey escape
being last year's bird – some feather in his cap!

Indeed this falcon was a sorry case,
more like a kestrel, it was such a small one.
It couldn't even take a finch, I guess.
If it missed once, or where the space was open,
taking more time would give no more success:
no, after a miss it would fly high for fun.
The reason that it lost the partridge there
was inattention: it had its mind elsewhere.

Just then a partridge broke and flew uphill:
Foglia saw; made an excellent launch at it.
The hawk came beating down the open field,
struck, and held on directly opposite.
Foglia bounds down the slope – a certain kill,
he thinks, because the hawk was made, and fit;
in a clear space, where there's not a stick of wood:
but on the ground, on beak and claws, just blood.

This is because the hawk's in its first feathers.
But all this while Oliver has been yelling,
'Call Cappellaio down, and call the others.
Look, one of them's here, look,' so he went on babbling,
'Tie up the dogs – Distaff will be enough for
this piece of work, he digs them out of hell.
Come down, Guglielmo, don't just stand and fiddle –
Combine with Foglia, catch it in the middle.'

Così fu fatto; e come sono in punto,
il canattier diceva: – Sotto, Rocca:
qui cadde, ve': e se tu l'arai giunto,
siasi tuo: corri qui; te', pogli bocca –.
Poi dice: – Avete voi guardato a punto? –
Ed in quel lo starnon del fondo scocca:
– Ecco a te, Foglia –. E 'l Foglia grida e getta,
e 'l simil fe' Guglielmo molto in fretta.

Lasciò la starna andarne lo sparvieri,
ed attende a fuggir quel che gli ha drieto:
disse Guglielmo: – Tu l'hai, Foglia Amieri –
e, benché nol dimostri, e' n'è pur lieto.
– Corri tu, che vi se' presso, Ulivieri –
diceva il Foglia; e Guglielmo sta cheto:
corse Ulivieri; e, come a loro è sceso,
vide che l'un sparviere ha l'altro preso.

Quel del Foglia avea preso per la gorga
quel di Guglielmo, e crede che 'l suo sia.
Par che a Guglielmo tal parole porga:
– La tua è stata pur gran villania:
non credo a starne lo sparviere scorga,
ma a sparvieri: egli è troppa pazzia
a impacciarsi uccellando con fanciulli:
questi non son buon giochi o buon trastulli –.

Guglielmo cheto sta, e gran fatica
dura a tener la letizia coperta;
pur con umil parole par che dica:
– Io nollo vidi, e questa è cosa certa –;
e questo più e più volte riplica.
Intanto il Foglia avea giù sceso l'erta;
e come alli sparvier fu prossimano,
quel di Guglielmo è guasto, e 'l suo è sano.

E getta presto il suo logoro in terra:
lo sparvier non men presto vi si pose:
e come a vincitor in quella guerra,
vezzi gli fa e assai piacevol cose.
Vede intanto Guglielmo che lui erra,
e 'l guasto è il suo sparviere; onde rispose
al Foglia: – Tu se' pur tu il villano –
e mancò poco non li die' con mano.

That's what they did, and when they were arranged,
the kennelman said, 'Distaff, get in under.
It fell there, look for it, and if you catch it,
it's yours – this way, run in, get your mouth round it.'
Then he asked the air: 'Did you mark the place exactly?'
Right through his words the partridge shoots in sight.
'It's all yours, Foglia.' Foglia yelled and threw,
and hastily Guglielmo launched his too.

The first hawk soon abandons their joint quarry
and tries to escape the danger on his tail.
'You've got her,' says Guglielmo to Amieri –
though he's delighted, he conceals his smile.
'Run after them, you're nearest, Oliver,'
calls Foglia, and Guglielmo keeps his counsel.
Oliver runs as bidden: when he's close,
he sees one hawk is in the other's claws.

Foglia's has got Guglielmo's by the throat,
but Foglia thinks it's his bird underneath.
So he turns on young Guglielmo in a bate:
'That is a villainous trick you've played on me –
I don't believe your falcon aims at prey but
at other falcons. Oh, I must be crazy
to mess with any hunt that kids go on.
This is no sport. This is no sort of fun.'

Guglielmo stands there quietly: with great efforts
he manages to stifle his amusement.
He even volunteers these humble words:
'I didn't see him go, I'm sure I didn't.'
This formula he several times repeats.
Foglia meantime is striding down the bank,
gets near the birds and sees for the first time
Guglielmo's hawk is wrecked and his is fine.

Quickly he throws his lure upon the ground.
His hawk as quickly comes and folds his wings.
And, like a fighter who had won that round,
he strokes it, hums, and tells it pleasant things.
On which Guglielmo sees that he saw wrong,
and that the wreck's his own, and so he flings
Foglia's word back: 'You were the villain then,'
and bunched his fists and almost gave him one.

Ma come il Foglia s'accorse dell'atto,
scostossi un poco, acciò che non li dessi.
Disse Guglielmo al Foglia: – Tu se' matto,
se ne credi andar netto; e s'io credessi
non far vendetta di quel che m'hai fatto,
credo m'impiccherei: e s'io avessi
meco Michel di Giorgio o 'l Vannuccino,
attenderesti ad altro, cervellino –.

Il Foglia innanzi alla furia si leva
e stassi cheto, ed ha pur pazienzia;
e altro viso e parole non aveva
quel che aspettando in favor la sentenzia,
e poi subitamente la perdeva.
Disse Guglielmo: – Io voglio usar prudenzia;
terrolla a mente in sino all'ore estreme,
e rivedremci qualche volta insieme –.

Già il sole in verso mezzogiorno cala
e vien l'ombre scemando che raccorcia;
dà lor proporzione e brutta e mala,
come a figura dipinta in iscorcia:
rinforzava il suo canto la cicala
e 'l mondo ardeva a guisa d'una torcia:
l'aria sta cheta ed ogni fronde salda
nella stagion più dispettosa e calda.

Quando il mio Dionigi tutto rosso,
sudando, come fussi un uovo fresco,
disse: – Star più con voi certo non posso:
deh vientene almen tu, Giovan Francesco!
Ma venitene tutti per ir grosso;
troppo sarebbe fiero barberesco
chi volessi or, quando la terra è accesa,
aspettar più per pascersi di presa –.

E detto questo, diè volta al cavallo
sanza aspettar Giovan Francesco ancora:
ciascun si mette presto a seguitallo,
ché 'l sol ciascun consumava e divora;
el Cappellaio vien drieto, e seguitâllo
e bracchi, ansando con la lingua fuora:
quanto più vanno, el caldo più raddoppia;
pare appiccato il fuoco in ogni stoppia.

But Foglia realised what was going to happen
and backed a little, to avoid a punch.
Guglielmo shouted at him, 'You're a madman
if you believe you'll get off this unpunished.
Believe me, Foglia, after what you've done,
I'll hang myself if I don't get revenge.
And if I'd little John here now, or Michael,
I'd give you something else to think of, fool!'

Faced with this fury, Foglia merely stands
and holds his peace and shows his kind of patience;
meaning he has the expression and the language
of one who expects a favourable judgement
and then is sent down suddenly, condemned.
Guglielmo says: 'I will avoid imprudence:
I'll keep this thing in mind till my last hour.
We'll meet again on this, some time, some where.'

Already the sun's at noon and pouring down,
and tops and tails the shadows that it shortens,
giving them ugly, evil disproportion,
like forms distorted when the brush foreshortens;
and the cicada sang a louder burden,
and the world blazed about us like a torch.
The air stood still and stiffened every leaf –
that pitiless time of heat without relief.

Now my Dionigi, who had gone all scarlet,
and glistening, like an egg that's just been peeled,
spoke up: 'I can't stay here another minute.
Won't you come too, Giovan Francesco? – please.
No, everyone come, and let the path be crowded –
it takes somebody savager than me
when the earth's lit and burning up, to wait
in hopes of catching something we can eat?'

After these words, he simply wheeled his horse
not waiting on Giovan Francesco any more.
We soon began to follow, all of us,
feeling the sun consuming and devouring.
Cappellaio came behind us with his braches
pursuing, panting, bringing their tongues before them.
As we come down the track, the heat is doubled;
a fire seems lit in every stubble field.

Tornonsi a casa chi tristo e chi lieto:
e chi ha pieno il carnaiuol di starne,
alcun si sta sanza esse, tristo e cheto,
e bisogna procacci d'altra carne:
Guglielmo vienne dispettoso a drieto,
né può di tanta ingiuria pace farne:
Giovan Francesco già non se ne cura,
ché uccella per piacer, non per natura.

E giunti a casa, riponeva il cuoio
e i can governa e mette nella stalla
el canattier: poi all'infrescatoio
truovasi ognun co' be' bicchieri a galla.
Quivi si fa un altro uccellatoio,
quivi le starne alcun non lascia o falla.
Pare trebbiano el vin, sendo cercone;
sì fa la voglia le vivande buone.

El primo assalto fu senza romore:
ognuno attende a menar le mascella;
ma poi, passato un po' il primo furore,
chi d'una cosa, chi d'altra favella;
ciascuno al suo sparvier dava l'onore,
cercando d'una scusa pronta e bella:
e chi molto non fe' con lo sparviere,
si sforza or qui col ragionare e bere.

Ogni cosa guastava la quistione
del Foglia con Guglielmo: onde si lieva
su Dionigi con buona intenzione,
e in questo modo a Guglielmo diceva:
– Vuo' tu tôrre tanta consolazione?
e benché il caso stran pur ti pareva,
fa' che tu sia, come son io, discreto,
che ammazzai il mio sparviere e stiemmi cheto –.

Queste parole e questo dolce stile,
perché Guglielmo l'ama, assai li piace;
e perché gli era pur di cor gentile,
diliberò col Foglia far la pace;
onde li disse con parole umile:
– Star più teco non voglio in contumace
e voglio in pace tutto sofferire –.
Fatto questo, ciascun vanne a dormire.

Some going home are sad and some are glad;
some have their gamebag full of partridges,
and some have nothing and are still and sad,
thinking they'll have to buy some other flesh.
Guglielmo hangs behind us, feeling bad –
he cannot bury such great injuries.
Giovan Francesco thinks of something else –
but then, he hunts to please us, not himself.

Back at the house, the master of our hounds
hangs up their leathers, sees to their rewards
and kennels them. Then everyone is found
by the cooler, brimming glasses in their hands.
Here there's another version of the hunt,
where no one misses or abandons birds.
The wine, though stale, could be Romagna's best –
and longing gives the food a gourmet taste.

The first attack on it was made in silence:
we wield our jawbones with great concentration.
Then, the first fury past, someone begins
to utter words, and soon we've conversation.
Each claims, for his own hawk, the best performance,
with quick excuses, and fair explanation,
and one who cut no figure with his hawk
now plays the champion in drink and talk.

One cloud darkens our sky, the argument
Guglielmo has with Foglia, which is why
Dionigi gets to his feet with good intent
and whispers to Guglielmo in this way:
'Don't throw away the comfort I present;
though the suggestion may appear outré,
follow the calm example that I set,
killing my falcon and then keeping quiet.'

These words, the new idea, the dulcet style,
from his beloved friend, attract and please
Guglielmo – and besides, his heart is noble;
so he decides that he will make the peace,
approaches Foglia, and his words are humble:
'I don't want to keep fighting you like this;
I want to live in peace and bear the loss.'
On this, we all retire to sleep it off.

E quel che si sognassi per la notte,
quello sarebbe bello a poter dire,
ch'io so ch'ognun rimetterà le dotte;
insino a terza vorranno dormire.
Poi ce n'andremo insieme a quelle grotte
e qualche lasca farem fuori uscire.
E così passò, o compar, lieto il tempo
con mille rime in zucchero ed a tempo.

LORENZO DE' MEDICI
(1449-92)

And what was dreamed of by the hunters then,
I wish that I could say, because I know
we'll all catch up on sleep we lost this morning –
we'll all want to lie in till nine or so.
After, the gang will go to the famous caverns
and from the cool depths draw a roach or two.
And so, my friend, we passed our happy time
with rhymes, sweet rhymes in sugar, keeping time.

LORENZO DE' MEDICI

Orlando Furioso

FROM *Canto I*

1

Le donne, i cavallier, l'arme, gli amori,
le cortesie, l'audaci imprese io canto,
che furo al tempo che passaro i Mori
d'Africa il mare, e in Francia nocquer tanto,
seguendo l'ire e i giovenil furori
d'Agramante lor re, che si diè vanto
di vendicar la morte di Troiano
sopra re Carlo imperator romano.

13-17

La donna il palafreno a dietro volta,
e per la selva a tutta briglia il caccia;
né per la rara più che per la folta,
la più sicura e miglior via procaccia:
ma pallida, tremando, e di sé tolta,
lascia cura al destrier che la via faccia.
Di su di giù, ne l'alta selva fiera
tanto girò, che venne a una riviera.

Su la riviera Ferraù trovosse
di sudor pieno e tutto polveroso.
Da la battaglia dianzi lo rimosse
un gran disio di bere e di riposo;
e poi, mal grado suo, quivi fermosse,
perché, de l'acqua ingordo e frettoloso,
l'elmo nel fiume si lasciò cadere,
né l'avea potuto anco riavere.

Quanto potea più forte, ne veniva
gridando la donzella ispaventata.
A quella voce salta in su la riva
il Saracino, e nel viso la guata;
e la conosce subito ch'arriva,
ben che di timor pallida e turbata,
e sien più dì che non n'udì novella,
che senza dubbio ell'è Angelica bella.

Orlando Furioso

1

Of ladies and of knights, arms and amours,
of courtesy and brave enterprise I sing,
which happened in that century when the Moors
from Africa to France came havocking,
bidden there in the mad and angry cause
of Agramant their young and boastful king,
who vowed to avenge his father's death, by war
on Charlemagne, the Roman emperor.

13-17

The lady turned her palfrey with the brid-
le and galloped reinless through the woods away,
nor did she try the safest route, to ride
where less rather than more obstruction lay –
but pale and shaking, shaken and beside
herself, she left the beast to pick their way.
So up and down through the wild foliage
she whirled, until she reached a river's edge.

There by the river's edge Ferraù knelt
sweating all over, powdery with dust,
who from the battle just before had felt
moved by a great desire to drink and rest,
and here against his will had been compelled
to stay: greedy for water and in haste
he'd dropped his helmet in the stream, and still
couldn't retrieve it from the chuckling rill.

With all her strength the damsel terrified
came screaming into view. The Saracen
at such a voice jumped out onto the side
and looked her in the face, a lovely one
he recognised as soon as she arrived,
though pale with fright and with her hair undone,
and though for days he'd heard no news of her:
it certainly was the fair Angelica.

E perché era cortese, e n'avea forse
non men dei dui cugini il petto caldo,
l'aiuto che potea tutto le porse,
pur come avesse l'elmo, ardito e baldo:
trasse la spada, e minacciando corse
dove poco di lui temea Rinaldo.
Più volte s'eran già non pur veduti,
m' al paragon de l'arme conosciuti.

Cominciar quivi una crudel battaglia,
come a piè si trovàr, coi brandi ignudi:
non che le piastre e la minuta maglia,
ma ai colpi lor non reggerian gl'incudi.
Or, mentre l'un con l'altro si travaglia,
bisogna al palafren che 'l passo studi;
che quanto può menar de le calcagna,
colei lo caccia al bosco e alla campagna.

So Ferraù, who had as warm a heart
as the two cousins, and was most well-bred,
bravely offered his help and took her part
as if he had his helmet on his head:
drew out his sword and made a menacing start
upon Rinaldo, who stood unafraid.
They knew each other fairly well by sight
and even by the experience of some fight.

Then they began a cruel combat there,
finding themselves on foot, with naked blades:
not metal suits or shirts of woven wire,
not even anvils could resist such hits.
Now while they spend their strength upon each other,
the palfrey has to mend its pace: for hard
as she can kick it with her little heels,
she drives it back into the woods and fields.

90-92

Mentre Ruggier di quella gente bella,
che per soccorrer Francia si prepara,
mira le varie insegne e ne favella,
e dei signor britanni i nomi impara;
uno et un altro a lui, per mirar quella
bestia sopra cui siede, unica o rara,
maraviglioso corre e stupefatto;
e tosto il cerchio intorno gli fu fatto.

Sì che per dare ancor più maraviglia,
e per pigliarne il buon Ruggier più gioco,
al volante corsier scuote la briglia,
e con gli sproni ai fianchi il tocca un poco:
quel verso il ciel per l'aria il camin piglia,
e lascia ognuno attonito in quel loco.
Quindi Ruggier, poi che di banda in banda
vide gl'Inglesi, andò verso l'Irlanda.

E vide Ibernia fabulosa, dove
il santo vecchiarel fece la cava,
in che tanta mercé par che si truove,
che l'uom vi purga ogni sua colpa prava.
Quindi poi sopra il mare il destrier muove
là dove la minor Bretagna lava;
e nel passar vide, mirando a basso,
Angelica legata al nudo sasso.

95

La fiera gente inospitale e cruda
alla bestia crudel nel lito espose
la bellissima donna, così ignuda
come Natura prima la compose.
Un velo non ha pure, in che richiuda
i bianchi gigli e le vermiglie rose,
da non cader per luglio o per dicembre,
di che son sparse le polite membre.

90-92

But while Ruggiero watched this fine parade
of help for France and saw the soldiers train,
and scanned their coats of arms and asked for aid
to learn the names of British gentlemen,
some of them came to him, where they surveyed
the beast on which he sat, a specimen
unique or rare, they wondered, all astounded;
and soon spectators had the pair surrounded.

So that, to make them marvel even more, the
jolly Ruggiero, to increase his sport,
shook at the bridle of his flying courser
and spurred its flanks to starboard and to port;
it trotted vertically up the ether
to the surprise of all St James's Court.
Then, as he'd seen the English here and there, he
ordered the hippogriff to fly to Eire.

He saw Hibernia, legendary ground,
which has the well dug by the little old saint,
in which they say heaven's grace does so abound
a man can clean himself of every taint.
And then he flew his steed across the sound
where the Channel washes Lesser Britain's feet;
and as he crossed, looked down and saw – my God! –
Angelica, bound, upon the naked rock.

95

That savage people, fierce to guests, and raw,
exposed the beautiful lady to the beast
and all its cruelties upon the shore
as naked as when Nature formed her first.
She had not even a veil on, to obscure
the snowy lilies and the scarlet roses –
they fall not in July nor yet December –
spread on the smooth patina of her members.

Il destrier punto, ponta i piè all'arena
e sbalza in aria, e per lo ciel galoppa;
e porta il cavalliero in su la schena,
e la donzella dietro in su la groppa.
Così privò la fera de la cena
per lei soave e delicata troppa.
Ruggier si va volgendo, e mille baci
figge nel petto e negli occhi vivaci.

Non più tenne la via, come propose
prima, di circundar tutta la Spagna;
ma nel propinquo lito il destrier pose,
dove entra in mar più la minor Bretagna.
Sul lito un bosco era di querce ombrose,
dove ognor par che Filomena piagna,
ch'in mezzo avea un pratel con una fonte,
e quinci e quindi un solitario monte.

Quivi il bramoso cavallier ritenne
l'audace corso, e nel pratel discese;
e fe' raccorre al suo destrier le penne,
ma non a tal che più le avea distese.
Del destrier sceso, a pena si ritenne
di salir altri; ma tennel l'arnese:
l'arnese il tenne, che bisognò trarre,
e contra il suo disir messe le sbarre.

Frettoloso, or da questo or da quel canto
confusamente l'arme si levava.
Non gli parve altra volta mai star tanto;
che s'un laccio sciogliea, dui n'annodava.
Ma troppo è lungo ormai, Signor, il canto,
e forse ch'anco l'ascoltar vi grava:
sì ch'io differirò l'istoria mia
in altro tempo che più grata sia.

LUDOVICO ARIOSTO
(1474-1533)

The charger, goaded, stamps its feet on the sand,
takes a spring in the air, and gallops upward,
carrying the knight upon its backbone and
the damsel right behind him on its croup.
So it deprived the monster of its planned
(but much too sweet and delicate for it) supper.
Ruggiero can't sit straight: half-turned he flies
kissing her breast and her reviving eyes.

He did not keep the route he had intended,
to circumnavigate the whole of Spain;
but on the nearby coast instead they landed,
where Brittany thrusts furthest into Ocean.
On the beach a grove of shady oaks was planted,
where Philomena sings her long complaint,
with, in the middle, a small field and a fountain,
and on each side a little lonely mountain.

Here Roger, chivalrous but full of longings,
stopped their bold flight and came down on the grass;
he made his charger fold its magic wings,
but his desire had wings he could not close.
Dismounting from one steed, he nearly flings
himself upon the other: his metal clothes
entangle him – he must get off this gear –
it puts a cage around his winged desire.

Confused between the right side and the wrong,
in haste he struggles from his heavy suit.
Before, he thought, this never took so long –
one lace would slacken, and two others knot.
But, Cardinal, I must prune this evening's song –
you will be weary of my weighty plot –
I shall postpone the next bit of my story
to another time, so it can please, not bore you.

LUDOVICO ARIOSTO

Gerusalemme Liberata, *Canto III*

Ali ha ciascuno al core ed ali al piede,
né del suo ratto andar però s'accorge:
ma, quando il sol gli aridi campi fiede
con raggi assai ferventi, e in alto sorge,
ecco apparir Gierusalem si vede,
ecco additar Gierusalem si scorge;
ecco da mille voci unitamente
Gierusalemme salutar si sente.

Così di naviganti audace stuolo,
che mova a ricercar estranio lido,
e in mar dubbioso e sotto ignoto polo
provi l'onde fallaci e 'l vento infido,
s'al fin discopre il desïato suolo,
il saluta da lunge in lieto grido;
e l'uno a l'altro il mostra, e in tanto oblia
la noia e 'l mal de la passata via.

Al gran piacer che quella prima vista
dolcemente spirò ne l'altrui petto,
alta contrizïon successe, mista
di timoroso e riverente affetto;
osano a pena d'inalzar la vista
ver' la città, di Cristo albergo eletto,
dove morì, dove sepolto fue,
dove poi rivestì le membra sue.

Sommessi accenti e tacite parole,
rotti singulti e flebili sospiri
de la gente ch'in un s'allegra e duole,
fan che per l'aria un mormorìo s'aggiri
qual ne le folte selve udir si suole,
s'avvien che tra le frondi il vento spiri;
o quale infra gli scogli, o presso a i lidi
sibila il mar percosso in rauchi stridi.

In Sight of Jerusalem

Their hearts have wings, they seem to have winged feet,
not noticing how fast they walk or ride;
but when the sun strikes the dry plains with heat
from his full burning rays and rises high,
there they can see Jerusalem appear,
there they point out Jerusalem in sight,
and there a thousand voices can be heard
greeting Jerusalem with one accord.

They are like sailors, like a daring band
of sea-explorers under unknown skies,
who cross strange seas to find a foreign strand
through the waves' tricks and the wind's perfidies,
and if at last they raise the longed-for land,
call to it in the distance with glad cries,
and help each other see it, and forget
the passage there, the trouble and the fret.

After the joy of that first sight, that vision
that in each heart so great a sweetness blows,
there came in turn a sense of deep contrition
and love so reverent and so timorous
the Crusaders hardly dare to lift their vision
towards that town (the shelter Jesus chose),
the parts he died in or was buried in,
and where he wore the body once again.

With lowered voices and with words not said,
with broken sobs and with the tearful sighs
of men who are both sorrowful and glad,
they stir the air around with muffled noise
of muttering, like the murmur in a wood
that flutters with the breathing of a breeze,
or as among the rocks or near the shores
the struck sea whistles, hoarsely grumbles, roars.

Nudo ciascun il piè calca il sentiero;
ché l'essempio de' duci ogn'altro move:
serico fregio o d'òr, piuma o cimiero
superbo, dal suo capo ognun rimove;
ed insieme del cor l'abito altero
depone: e calde e pie lagrime piove:
pur, quasi al pianto abbia la via rinchiusa,
così parlando ognun sé stesso accusa:

– Dunque, ove tu, Signor, di mille rivi
sanguinosi il terren lasciasti asperso,
d'amaro pianto almen duo fonti vivi
in sì acerba memoria oggi io non verso?
Agghiacciato mio cor, ché non derivi
per gli occhi, e stilli in lagrime converso?
Duro mio cor, ché non ti spetri e frangi?
Pianger ben merti ognor, s'ora non piangi. –

Da la cittade in tanto un ch'a la guarda
sta d'alta torre, e scopre i monti e i campi,
colà giuso la polve alzarsi guarda,
sì che par che gran nube in aria stampi:
par che baleni quella nube ed arda,
come di fiamme gravida e di lampi:
poi lo splendor de' lucidi metalli
distingue, e scerne gli uomini e i cavalli.

TORQUATO TASSO
(1544-95)

Barefoot they tread the surface of the road,
for the example of their leaders moves them;
if they had silk adornments, plumes or gold,
or proudly crested helmets, they remove them;
and even the inner habit of the proud
heart they put off: warm pious tears come pouring;
and yet, as if they'd blocked up lamentation,
they blame themselves with open accusation:

'So on this holy ground, dear Lord, which You
left scattered with a thousand streams of blood,
can I not pour that bitter memory two
small living streams of mourning from my head?
O heart of ice, can you not melt into
my eyes and flow transformed to tears instead?
Crack now, hard heart, weep now, my rocky core –
or you'll deserve to weep for evermore.'

In the city meantime, someone in a tower
on lookout scanning hills and plains makes out
down there some dust rising from somewhere lower
until it marks the air as a great cloud,
and this appears to flash inside and flare
pregnant with flaming and pulsating light;
at last he sees the glinting and the sheen
is metal, and it's horses there and men.

TORQUATO TASSO
Jerusalem Unbound, Canto III, 3-9.

51

Gerusalemme Liberata, *Canto XII*

Io piangendo ti presi, e in breve cesta
fuor ti portai, tra fiori e frondi ascosa:
ti celai da ciascun, che né di questa
diedi sospizïon, né d'altra cosa:
me n'andai sconosciuto; e per foresta
camminando di piante orride ombrosa,
vidi una tigre, che minaccie ed ire
avea ne gli occhi, in contr'a me venire.

Sovra un arbore i' salsi, e te su l'erba
lasciai; tanta paura il cor mi prese.
Giunse l'orribil fèra, e, la superba
testa volgendo, in te lo sguardo intese;
mansuefece, e raddolcìo l'acerba
vista con atto placido e cortese;
lenta poi s'avvicina, e ti fa vezzi
con la lingua: e tu ridi, e l'accarezzi;

ed ischerzando seco, al fèro muso
la pargoletta man secura stendi.
Ti porge ella le mamme, e come è l'uso
di nutrice s'adatta, e tu le prendi.
In tanto io miro, timido e confuso,
come uom farìa novi prodigi orrendi.
Poi che sazia ti vede omai la belva
del suo latte, ella parte e si rinselva...

TORQUATO TASSO

Clorinda Smuggled Out of Ethiopia

In tears I took you up, in a small basket
carried you out, hidden in leaves and flowers;
let no one see; did nothing to direct
suspicion to this act or any other;
and got away unnoticed. As I walked
through jungle shadowy with savage verdure,
I saw a tiger coming, that we'd meet,
and in its eyes it had an angry threat.

I climbed a tree: I'd put you on the ground
and left you, overtaken by such fear...
The terrible beast came up, and, turning round
its haughty head, it aimed its looks at yours;
then tamed and put some sweetness in its sour
aspect, with peaceful courteous behaviour:
slowly it bent down closer and caressed
you with its tongue: you laughed and tried to kiss it,

and you stretched out your little hand in play
to its ferocious muzzle, quite untroubled.
It offered you its teats, and in the way
of nurses, nestled till you got a hold.
Meanwhile I watched, like a man shocked and shy,
who watches awful miracles, and marvelled.
When the beast saw you full of milk at last,
it parted from you, back into its forest...

Torquato Tasso
Jerusalem Unbound, Canto XII, 29-31.

Gerusalemme Liberata, *Canto XIV*

Qual cauta cacciatrice, Armida aspetta
Rinaldo al varco. Ei su l'Oronte giunge,
ove un rio si dirama, e, un'isoletta
formando, tosto a lui si ricongiunge;
e 'n su la riva una colonna eretta
vede, e un picciol battello indi non lunge.
Fisa egli tosto gli occhi al bel lavoro
del bianco marmo, e legge in lettre d'oro:

– O chiunque tu sia, che voglia o caso
peregrinando adduce a queste sponde,
maraviglie maggior l'orto o l'occaso
non ha di ciò che l'isoletta asconde.
Passa, se vuoi vederla. – È persuaso
tosto l'incauto a girne oltra quell'onde;
e, perché mal capace era la barca,
gli scudieri abbandona, ed ei sol varca.

Come è là giunto, cupido e vagante
volge intorno lo sguardo, e nulla vede,
fuor ch'antri ed acque e fiori ed erbe e piante;
onde quasi schernito esser si crede:
ma pur quel loco è così lieto, e in tante
guise l'alletta, ch'ei si ferma e siede,
e disarma la fronte, e la ristaura
al soave spirar di placid'aura.

Il fiume gorgogliar fra tanto udìo
con novo suono; e là con gli occhi corse:
e mover vide un'onda in mezzo al rio
che in sé stessa si volse e si ritorse;
e quinci alquanto d'un crin biondo uscio,
e quinci di donzella un vólto sorse,
e quinci il petto e le mammelle, e de la
sua forma in fin dove vergogna cela.

Così dal palco di notturna scena
o ninfa o dea, tarda sorgendo, appare.
Questa, benché non sia vera Sirena
ma sia magica larva, una ben pare
di quelle che già presso a la tirrena
piaggia abitâr l'insidïoso mare;

Armida Enchanted with Rinaldo

As wary as a hunter, Armida waits
for Rinaldo at that ford. The Orontes river
unbraids there, forms an island, and replaits
the strings of water round it. He arrives
and on the bank he sees a little boat's
drawn up; nearby a column has been carved.
His eyes are caught by the fine workmanship
of the white marble; he reads the gold inscription:

'Whoever you may be, whom choice or chance
has brought upon your wanderings to this beach,
this island holds a marvel that the lands
of sunrise and of sunset cannot match.
Cross if you wish to see.' These words convince
the knight he wants to cross the waves: he's rash,
there's not much room in the small skiff... He leaves
his squires and passes over by himself.

On the other side he turns his keen and venturous
looks all around him: nothing is in sight
but caves and waters, grasses, shrubs, and flowers,
so that he thinks perhaps it was a cheat;
and yet the place entices him and cheers
him so, that he stops walking and just sits,
unarms his face and forehead and refreshes
his brow in the smooth-breathing peaceful breeze.

While doing this, he hears the river babble
with a new sound; and quickly moves his eyes
and sees there is a wave out in the middle
turning itself and twisting in strange ways;
there a blond tress emerges from the tumble,
and here a face, a girl's face, seems to rise,
and there's her chest, her breasts, and so she rides
up in the water to the point shame hides.

It's like an appearance on the stage, a nymph
or goddess slowly rising till she's on.
This creature's nothing but a magic phantom,
not a real Siren, but she does seem one
of those who used to lie in watery ambush
just off the coast of the Tyrrhenian:

né men ch'in viso bella, in suono è dolce
e così canta, e 'l cielo e l'aure molce:

– O giovanetti, mentre aprile e maggio
v'ammantan di fiorite e verdi spoglie,
di gloria e di virtù fallace raggio
la tenerella mente ah non v'invoglie!
solo chi segue ciò che piace è saggio,
e in sua stagion degli anni il frutto coglie.
Questo grida natura. Or dunque voi
indurarete l'alma a i detti suoi?

Folli, perché gettate il caro dono,
che breve è sì, di vostra età novella?
Nome, e senza soggetto idoli sono
ciò che pregio e valore il mondo appella.
La fama che invaghisce a un dolce suono
voi superbi mortali, e par sì bella,
è un'eco, un sogno, anzi del sogno un'ombra,
ch'ad ogni vento si dilegua e sgombra.

Goda il corpo securo, e in lieti oggetti
l'alma tranquilla appaghi i sensi frali:
oblii le noie andate, e non affretti
le sue miserie in aspettando i mali.
Nulla curi se 'l ciel tuoni o saetti:
minacci egli a sua voglia, e infiammi strali;
questo è saver, questa è felice vita:
sì l'insegna natura, e sì l'addita. –

Sì canta l'empia; e 'l giovenetto al sonno
con note invoglia sì soavi e scorte.
Quel serpe a poco a poco, e si fa donno
sovra i sensi di lui possente e forte:
né i tuoni omai destar, non ch'altro, il ponno
da quella queta imagine di morte.
Esce d'aguato allor la falsa maga,
e gli va sopra, di vendetta vaga.

Ma quando in lui fissò lo sguardo, e vide
come placido in vista egli respira,
e ne' begli occhi un dolce atto che ride,
ben che sian chiusi (or che fia s'ei li gira?),
pria s'arresta sospesa, e gli s'asside
poscia vicina, e placar sente ogn'ira

she's fair of face and no less sweet in sound,
and sings like this, and soothes the sky and wind:

'Young men, young men, while April still and May
dress you in coats of flowers and greenery,
keep off your tender minds the treacherous ray
of ardent manliness and arid glory!
The wise all follow pleasure – only they
are wise, and pick the fruits of time when ready.
Nature cries out this truth – Are you so hard
of heart and hearing to your mother's word?

Why throw away your dearest gift, you fools,
your time of spring, that lasts so short a time?
What the world calls esteem and worth are idols –
mere names – and no one really worships them.
This fame, which sounds so sweet to you proud mortals
you fall in love with it, so fair it seems –
fame is an echo, a dream, no a shadow in a
dream that each breath of wind spreads ever thinner.

Let body, carefree, take its joy; and soul
calmly appease frail sense with happiness.
Forget past trouble and avoid the pall
that forethought casts, of coming miseries.
Let heaven thunder, let its lightning fall;
ignore its missiles and its menaces.
This is the happy life and being wise.
This nature teaches, this is her advice.'

So wickedly she sang; and he was stroked
to sleep by skilful song and honeyed breath.
It crept upon him like a snake and took
dominion of his senses from the youth.
Not even thunder, much less words, could wake
him from that image of untroubled death.
Then out of hiding comes the witch who tricked him
and wild for vengeance stands above her victim.

But when she's fixed her looks on him and seen
how peacefully he lies and breathes out peace,
and how in his fine eyes sweet smiles begin,
though they are shut (what if he turns his eyes?) –
first she stops still, hanging in doubt, and then
sits by him, feeling all her anger pass

mentre il risguarda; e 'n su la vaga fronte
pende omai sì, che par Narciso al fonte.

E quei ch'ivi sorgean vivi sudori
accoglie lievemente in un suo velo;
e, con un dolce ventillar, gli ardori
gli va temprando de l'estivo cielo.
Così (chi 'l crederìa?) sopiti ardori
d'occhi nascosi distemprâr quel gelo
che s'indurava al cor più che diamante:
e, di nemica, ella divenne amante.

Di ligustri, di gigli, e de le rose
le quai fiorìan per quelle piaggie amene,
con nov'arte congiunte, indi compose
lente ma tenacissime catene.
Queste al collo, a le braccia, a i piè gli pose;
così l'avvinse, e così preso il tiene:
quinci, mentr'egli dorme, il fa riporre
sovra un suo carro; e ratta il ciel trascorre.

Né già ritorna di Damasco al regno,
né dove ha il suo castello in mezzo a l'onde;
ma, ingelosita di sì caro pegno,
e vergognosa del suo amor s'asconde
ne l'oceàno immenso, ove alcun legno
rado, o non mai, va de le nostre sponde,
fuor tutti i nostri lidi; e quivi eletta
per solinga sua stanza è un'isoletta.

Un'isoletta la qual nome prende
con le vicine sue da la Fortuna.
Quinci ella in cima a una montagna ascende
disabitata, e d'ombre oscura e bruna;
e per incanto a lei nevose rende
le spalle e i fianchi, e senza neve alcuna
gli lascia il capo verdeggiante e vago;
e vi fonda un palagio appresso un lago;

ove in perpetuo april molle amorosa
vita seco ne mena il suo diletto...

TORQUATO TASSO

58

as she stares down; till, like Narcissus, now
she hangs reflecting on his pretty brow.

And softly dabbing with a veil of hers
she catches up his running drops of sweat:
and with a sweetly shaken fan she tempers
the ardours of the eastern summer heat,
so that (who would believe it?) the quenched ardours
of hidden eyes soon melt the frozen knot
that hardened in her heart like diamond:
and from an enemy she becomes a lover.

With privet-flowers, with lilies and with roses
which blossomed here and there in that pleasance,
she forges magic links and so composes
flexible, yielding but tenacious chains.
She winds them round his neck, his waist, his toes,
she ties him till she has him in her hands:
then calls her chariot; still asleep, she loads
him on; and flies along the heavenly roads.

Now she goes back, not to the Syrian palace,
nor to the Dead Sea where she has her castle;
but bashful of her love, already jealous
for her dear hostage, hastens to conceal
both of them in huge Ocean, where no galleys
ever or rarely from our harbours sail,
beyond our human limits; the asylum
she chooses is a little lonely island.

A little island in a group which took
from lady Fortune its attractive name.
The chariot lifted to a mountain peak
empty of people, shadowy and dim.
By magic she made snow and made it stick
over its flanks and shoulders, but the summit
left snowless, green and pretty – there she founds
a palazzo with a lago in its grounds.

There in perpetual April her delight
leads the soft life of love with her...

TORQUATO TASSO
Jerusalem Unbound, Canto XIV, 57-71.

Modo di filosofare

Il mondo è il libro dove il Senno Eterno
scrisse i proprii concetti, e vivo tempio
dove, pingendo i gesti e 'l proprio esempio,
di statue vive ornò l'imo e 'l superno;

perch'ogni spirto qui l'arte e 'l governo
leggere e contemplar, per non farsi empio,
debba, e dir possa: – Io l'universo adempio,
Dio contemplando a tutte cose interno. –

Ma noi, strette alme a' libri e tempii morti,
copïati dal vivo con più errori,
gli anteponghiamo a magistero tale.
O pene, del fallir fatene accorti,
liti, ignoranze, fatiche e dolori:
deh, torniamo, per Dio, all'originale!

Tommaso Campanella
(1568-1639)

The Way to Love Wisdom

The world's a book, the youthful diary
of the eternal Wisdom where he wrote
his thoughts; the living temple where he cut
his likenesses, to decorate earth and sky.

The aim was, every spirit should read there
and looking at his art and power, improve
themselves, till they could say: 'I finish off
his work, by seeing his image everywhere.'

But tied to books and temples that are mortal
(copied from life with many a mistake),
we prefer these to the Maker and the Model.
O pain, teach us our lesson: we are weak.
Illness and ignorance, save us: for God's sake,
we must go back to the original Book.

TOMMASO CAMPANELLA

Italia, Italia

Italia, Italia, o tu, cui feo la sorte
  Dono infelice di bellezza, ond' hai
  Funesta dote d'infiniti guai,
  Che in fronte scritti per gran doglia porte,
Deh, fossi tu men bella, o almen più forte,
  Onde assai più ti paventasse, o assai
  T'amasse men chi del tuo bello ai rai
  Par che si strugga, e pur ti sfida a morte!

Ch'or giù dall' Alpi non vedrei torrenti
  Scender d'armati, e del tuo sangue tinta
  Bever l'onda del Po gallici armenti.
Nè te vedrei del non tuo ferro cinta
  Pugnar col braccio di straniere genti,
  Per servir sempre o vincitrice o vinta.

VINCENZO DA FILICAIA
(1642-?1707)

Italia, Italia

O Italy, Italy, to whom Fate gave
The unhappy gift of beauty, which has meant
A deadly dowry that you bear engraved
Upon your brow, of infinite lament.
If you were just less beautiful, or just
So strong they feared you more or loved you less,
These lovers, who appear to melt with lust
But fight till they destroy your loveliness! –

Then from the Alps I would not see this flood
Of armed men pouring and the herds from Gaul
Drinking your river reddened with your blood.
Nor would I see you in your battles use
Strange swords, and arms of anyone at all –
To be a slave, whether you win or lose.

VINCENZO DA FILICAIA

A Zacinto

Nè più mai toccherò le sacre sponde
ove il mio corpo fanciulletto giacque,
Zacinto mia, che te specchi nell'onde
del greco mar, da cui vergine nacque

Venere e fêa quell'isole feconde
col suo primo sorriso, onde non tacque
le tue limpide nubi e le tue fronde
l'inclito verso di colui, che l'acque

cantò fatali, ed il diverso esiglio,
per cui bello di fama e di sventura
baciò la sua petrosa Itaca Ulisse.

Tu non altro che il canto avrai del figlio,
o materna mia terra; a noi prescrisse
il fato illacrimata sepoltura.

UGO FOSCOLO
(1778-1827)

To Zante

Nor shall I touch again the sacred margin
Of Zante where my small boy-body lay
When I was born, near waves that mirror Zante
In the Greek sea that Venus as a virgin

Was born from, giving such fertility
With her first smile to these Ionian islands,
Whose see-through clouds and woods escaped from silence
Thanks to the singer of the Odyssey –

That song of waters, exile, travel, fate,
In which the famous hero of distress
Kissed rocky Ithaca on arriving home.

You, mother Zante, from your son will get
Only the song; for Fate wrote down for us
Mere burial, with no mourners and no tomb.

UGO FOSCOLO

Er viaggio all'estro

Forzi sarà bucía, ma quarchiduno
che sta in artis e crede de sapello
dice ch'ar Papa je va p' er cervello
d'ugne le rote e scarrozzà a Belluno.

Bravo! farà benissimo; e gnisuno
pò negaje ch'un viaggio come quello
è sempre mejo che de stà a Castello
a pescacce le tinche p' er diggiuno.

Quadrini n'ha d'avanzo: passaporto
se lo firma da sé: dunque ha raggione,
e accidenti a lui chi je dà torto.

Eppoi, quer tornà Papa tra perzone
che t'hanno visto cicorietta d'orto
dev'èsse un gran gustaccio buggiarone.

[26 maggio 1835]

GIUSEPPE GIOACHINO BELLI
(1791-1863)

Travelling Abroad for a Bit

Could be a lie, but someone who should know,
A chap high up the ladder, says he feels
The Pope has it in mind to grease the wheels
And take his carriage out to see Belluno.

Great! – that's an excellent scheme; and who could cast
Aspersions on a jaunt like that, less sinful
Than hanging round all summer at Gandolfo
Fishing for tench so he can keep his fast.

Cash, he's got plenty; passport, well, he signs
His own: the whole thing makes a lot of sense –
And the devil take anyone who repines.

And then, to go back Pope among the dense
Buggers who saw you as a bit of a drip...
Now that must make a bloody marvellous trip.

[26 May 1835]

Giuseppe Gioachino Belli

Li malincontri

M'aricordo quann'ero piccinino
che tata me portava for de porta
a riccoje er grespigno, e quarche vorta
a rinfrescacce co un bicchier de vino.

Be', un giorno pe la strada de la Storta,
dov'è quelo sfasciume d'un casino,
ce trovassimo stesa lí vicino
tra un orticheto una regazza morta.

Tata, ar vedella lí a panza per aria
piena de sangue e co 'no squarcio in gola,
fece un strillo e pijò l'erba fumaria.

E io, sibbè tant'anni sò passati,
nun ho potuto più sentí parola
de girà pe li loghi scampagnati.

[15 aprile 1846]

GIUSEPPE GIOACHINO BELLI

Unlucky Encounters

I remember, when I was very tiny,
Dad used to take me out the gate of Rome
To pick some curly salad – and even some
Times to refresh us with a glass of wine.

Well, one day, on the Cassia, the tenth mile
Or so, where there's that house beside the track
In ruins, we found stretched out there round the back,
Plump in a patch of nettles, a dead girl.

Seeing her lying belly to the air
Covered in blood, with a hole across her neck,
Dad gave a squawk and took off out of there.

Though that was years ago – and 'time effaces' –
I still won't hear of going for a walk
In any of those lonely country places.

[15 April 1846]

GIUSEPPE GIOACHINO BELLI

L'infinito

Sempre caro mi fu quest'ermo colle,
e questa siepe, che da tanta parte
dell'ultimo orizzonte il guardo esclude.
Ma sedendo e mirando, interminati
spazi di là da quella, e sovrumani
silenzi, e profondissima quiete
io nel pensier mi fingo; ove per poco
il cor non si spaura. E come il vento
odo stormir tra queste piante, io quello
infinito silenzio a questa voce
vo comparando: e mi sovvien l'eterno,
e le morte stagioni, e la presente
e viva, e il suon di lei. Così tra questa
immensità s'annega il pensier mio:
e il naufragar m'è dolce in questo mare.

GIACOMO LEOPARDI
(1798-1837)

The Infinite

Always this baldly solitary hill
was dear to me; and this hedge too, that shuts
so much of the last horizon from one's sight.
But sitting here and staring out, I form
in thought unending spaces there behind it,
higher-than-human silences, and deep
beyond, the deepest peace; in which the heart
all but gives in to fear. And as I listen
to the wind bustling among these plants, I start
comparing this vociferation to
that infinite silence, and I call to mind
eternity, those dead seasons, and this present
and living one, and how it sounds. This way
in that immensity my thought is drowned:
and it is sweet to shipwreck in this sea.

GIACOMO LEOPARDI

La sera del dì di festa

Dolce e chiara è la notte e senza vento,
e queta sovra i tetti e in mezzo agli orti
posa la luna, e di lontan rivela
serena ogni montagna. O donna mia,
già tace ogni sentiero, e pei balconi
rara traluce la notturna lampa:
tu dormi, che t'accolse agevol sonno
nelle tue chete stanze; e non ti morde
cura nessuna; e già non sai né pensi
quanta piaga m'apristi in mezzo al petto.
Tu dormi: io questo ciel, che sì benigno
appare in vista, a salutar m'affaccio,
e l'antica natura onnipossente,
che mi fece all'affanno. A te la speme
nego, mi disse, anche la speme; e d'altro
non brillin gli occhi tuoi se non di pianto.
Questo dì fu solenne: or da' trastulli
prendi riposo; e forse ti rimembra
in sogno a quanti oggi piacesti, e quanti
piacquero a te: non io, non già, ch'io speri,
al pensier ti ricorro. Intanto io chieggo
quanto a viver mi resti, e qui per terra
mi getto, e grido, e fremo. Oh giorni orrendi
in così verde etate! Ahi, per la via
odo non lunge il solitario canto
dell'artigian, che riede a tarda notte,
dopo i sollazzi, al suo povero ostello;
e fieramente mi si stringe il core,
a pensar come tutto al mondo passa,
e quasi orma non lascia. Ecco è fuggito
il dì festivo, ed al festivo il giorno
volgar succede, e se ne porta il tempo
ogni umano accidente. Or dov'è il suono
di que' popoli antichi? or dov'è il grido
de' nostri avi famosi, e il grande impero
di quella Roma, e l'armi, e il fragorio
che n'andò per la terra e l'oceano?
Tutto è pace e silenzio, e tutto posa
il mondo, e più di lor non si ragiona.

The Evening of the Feast Day

The night is soft and clear, and there's no wind,
And calm on roofs and down inside the gardens
The moon rests, and uncovers in the distance,
Without a cloud, each mountain. O my lady,
Now every path is silent; only here
And there, through balconies, a last lamp shines:
You are asleep – drowsiness easily caught you
Among your quiet rooms; and not one care
Gnaws at you; now you neither know nor wonder
How great a wound you opened in my heart.
You sleep: while I lean out to greet this sky,
This heaven, which has tonight so kind a look,
And ancient nature, the almighty power
That moulded me for grief: for hope, it told me,
I here deny you – even hope: your eyes
Must never shine with anything but tears.
Today was festival: now from that enjoyment
You take your rest, and maybe you recall
In dreams how many you have pleased, how many
Pleased you today – I never, not that I hope,
Run there among your thoughts. Meantime I ask
How long I've left to live, and throw myself
On the ground, to moan and shiver. Horrible days
For my green years! But listen, from the street
I hear not far away the lonely singing
Of a workman going home from his amusements
In the late night, relieved, to his poor house;
And a wild anguish grips my heart, to think
How everything that's in the world goes by
And hardly leaves a trace. Look how this day
Of festival flowed away, how common day
Succeeds to special day, and time bears off
All man's events to nothing. Where is now
The noise that ancient peoples made? the cry
Of our own famous forbears? and where now
That empire of great Rome, the arms, the clash
Once heard expanding over land and sea?
All now is peace and silence, the world rests
Entirely, and no more is said of them.

Nella mia prima età, quando s'aspetta
bramosamente il dì festivo, or poscia
ch'egli era spento, io doloroso, in veglia,
premea le piume; ed alla tarda notte
un canto che s'udia per li sentieri
lontanando morire a poco a poco,
già similmente mi stringeva il core.

GIACOMO LEOPARDI

In my first youth, that time when one looks forward
With such desire to days of festival, after
The day was finished, I would lie in pain
Awake upon the feathers; late at night
A song that could be heard along some path
Dying by steps away into the distance
Would grip my heart with anguish just like this.

GIACOMO LEOPARDI

La ginestra
o Il fiore del deserto

E gli uomini vollero piuttosto le tenebre
che la luce.

GIOVANNI, 3, 19.

Qui su l'arida schiena
del formidabil monte
sterminator Vesevo,
la qual null'altro allegra arbor né fiore,
tuoi cespi solitari intorno spargi,
odorata ginestra,
contenta dei deserti. Anco ti vidi
de' tuoi steli abbellir l'erme contrade
che cingon la cittade
la qual fu donna de' mortali un tempo,
e del perduto impero
par che col grave e taciturno aspetto
faccian fede e ricordo al passeggero.
Or ti riveggo in questo suol, di tristi
lochi e dal mondo abbandonati amante,
e d'afflitte fortune ognor compagna.
Questi campi cosparsi
di ceneri infeconde, e ricoperti
dell'impietrata lava,
che sotto i passi al peregrin risona;
dove s'annida e si contorce al sole
la serpe, e dove al noto
cavernoso covil torna il coniglio;
fûr liete ville e colti,
e biondeggiâr di spiche, e risonâro
di muggito d'armenti;
fûr giardini e palagi,
agli ozi de' potenti
gradito ospizio; e fûr città famose
che coi torrenti suoi l'altero monte
dall'ignea bocca fulminando oppresse
con gli abitanti insieme. Or tutto intorno
una ruina involve,
dove tu siedi, o fior gentile, e quasi
i danni altrui commiserando, al cielo

Flowering Broom
or The Flower of the Desert

And men wanted darkness
rather than light.
JOHN, 3, 19.

Here on the arid spine
of the terrifying killer
mountain Vesuvius,
with not one other tree or flower to cheer us,
you scatter round your solitary tufts,
fragrant and flowering broom,
contented with a desert. I've also seen you
with your green stems brightening lonely stretches
of the campagna round
the City that was queen of mortals once –
places that with their grave and silent look
bear witness and remind
the traveller of the empire that was lost.
Now on this ground we meet again, you lover
of gloomy sites abandoned by the world,
faithful companion of all stricken fortunes.
These fields that have been scattered
with sterile cinders and been covered over
with lava turned to stone
that echoes under the stranger's pressing steps –
here, where the snake nests or coils in the sun,
and where the rabbit comes
home to its little cave, the familiar burrow –
were happy farms or hamlets; this was ploughland.
These fields grew blond with corn; the echoes were
of lowing from their herds;
here were gardens and palaces,
sheltering pleasantly
the leisure of the great; and famous cities,
which with its burning torrents the haughty mountain,
flickering lightning from its fiery mouth,
suppressed, with all their citizens. Now for miles
one common ruin wraps them,
where you, soft flower, are rooted, and as if
in pity of another's loss, to heaven

di dolcissimo odor mandi un profumo,
che il deserto consola. A queste piagge
venga colui che d'esaltar con lode
il nostro stato ha in uso, e vegga quanto
è il gener nostro in cura
all'amante natura. E la possanza
qui con giusta misura
anco estimar potrà dell'uman seme,
cui la dura nutrice, ov'ei men teme,
con lieve moto in un momento annulla
in parte, e può con moti
poco men lievi ancor subitamente
annichilare in tutto.
Dipinte in queste rive
son dell'umana gente
le magnifiche sorti e progressive.

Qui mira e qui ti specchia,
secol superbo e sciocco,
che il calle insino allora
dal risorto pensier segnato innanti
abbandonasti, e vòlti addietro i passi,
del ritornar ti vanti,
e procedere il chiami.
Al tuo pargoleggiar gl'ingegni tutti,
di cui lor sorte rea padre ti fece,
vanno adulando, ancora
ch'a ludibrio talora
t'abbian fra sé. Non io
con tal vergogna scenderò sotterra;
ma il disprezzo piuttosto che si serra
di te nel petto mio,
mostrato avrò quanto si possa aperto:
ben ch'io sappia che obblio
preme chi troppo all'età propria increbbe.
Di questo mal, che teco
mi fia comune, assai finor mi rido.
Libertà vai sognando, e servo a un tempo
vuoi di novo il pensiero,
sol per cui risorgemmo
dalla barbarie in parte, e per cui solo
si cresce in civiltà, che sola in meglio
guida i pubblici fati.

send up a perfume of the sweetest smell,
consoling all the desert round. Let those
who like to praise the happy state of man
come to these sloping hills and see how much
our kind is in the hands
of loving nature. Here with greater justice
they can assess the power of our seed,
whose heartless nourisher, when we're least afraid,
can lightly in a moment cancel us
in part or with a slightly
less easy movement in another second
wipe us out altogether.
Depicted on this spot
in stone the extent is reckoned
of man's 'magnificent and progressive lot'.

O proud and foolish age,
look at your image here:
see, you have left the path
renascent thought marked out in front of you
till now, and turned your steps toward the past –
you boast of going back
and call it progress. Childish
babble, to which the intellects unlucky
to be the children of your generation
listen with flattery, though
they jeer at you sometimes
among themselves. But I
shall not bear shame like that into my grave:
instead the deep contempt I lock inside
the hollow of my heart
I mean to show, as openly as one can –
although I know oblivion
lies heavy on those who dare displease their time.
This destiny, which I share
with you, my century, I can laugh at still.
You dream of Liberty, but you also want
to enslave man's thought again –
free thought, the only way
we rose a step from being barbarous,
our only way to reach civility,
which guides all peoples to a better fate.

Così ti spiacque il vero
dell'aspra sorte e del depresso loco
che natura ci die'. Per questo il tergo
vigliaccamente rivolgesti al lume
che il fe' palese: e, fuggitivo, appelli
vil chi lui segue, e solo
magnanimo colui
che sé schernendo o gli altri, astuto o folle,
fin sopra gli astri il mortal grado estolle.

Uom di povero stato e membra inferme
che sia dell'alma generoso ed alto,
non chiama sé né stima
ricco d'or né gagliardo,
e di splendida vita o di valente
persona infra la gente
non fa risibil mostra;
ma sé di forza e di tesor mendico
lascia parer senza vergogna, e noma
parlando, apertamente, e di sue cose
fa stima al vero uguale.
Magnanimo animale
non credo io già, ma stolto,
quel che nato a perir, nutrito in pene,
dice, a goder son fatto,
e di fetido orgoglio
empie le carte, eccelsi fati e nove
felicità, quali il ciel tutto ignora,
non pur quest'orbe, promettendo in terra
a popoli che un'onda
di mar commosso, un fiato
d'aura maligna, un sotterraneo crollo
distrugge sì, che avanza
a gran pena di lor la rimembranza.
Nobil natura è quella
che a sollevar s'ardisce
gli occhi mortali incontra
al comun fato, e che con franca lingua,
nulla al ver detraendo,
confessa il mal che ci fu dato in sorte,
e il basso stato e frale;
quella che grande e forte

So much you hated hearing
the truth of our harsh lot and the low place
that nature set us in. That's why you cowards
have turned your backs upon the light, for making
the truth so plain; and cringing, you cry down
the seekers of that light
and only treat as heroes
those who, with self-contempt or irony, place
above the stars (and praise) this mortal race.

The man of poor low state and weakly limbs,
if he is high and noble in his heart,
will neither think nor speak of
himself as rich or handsome,
and does not make a ludicrous exhibition
of glittering life or splendid
figure among his neighbours;
but lets his lack of strength and wealth, his need,
appear without false shame, and names it too
in conversation, openly, and reckons
his worth at its true rate.
I think that man a fool,
not a heroic spirit,
who, made for death, fed in the midst of pain,
cries, 'I was born to pleasure',
and fills with stinking pride
the pages of his books, promising here
on earth exalted fates and novel kinds
of happiness unknown in heaven itself,
let alone this poor globe,
to peoples that a wave
of the stirred sea, a breath
of evil air, a shrug beneath the ground
destroys so thoroughly
they only just survive in memory.
The truly noble nature
can take the risk of raising
our mortal eyes to face
the common fate and then can frankly and freely,
not censoring the truth,
admit the hand of destiny dealt us ill,
a low and feeble state;
in suffering he shows

mostra sé nel soffrir, né gli odii e l'ire
fraterne, ancor più gravi
d'ogni altro danno, accresce
alle miserie sue, l'uomo incolpando
del suo dolor, ma dà la colpa a quella
che veramente è rea, che de' mortali
madre è di parto e di voler matrigna.
Costei chiama inimica; e incontro a questa
congiunta esser pensando,
siccome è il vero, ed ordinata in pria
l'umana compagnia,
tutti fra sé confederati estima
gli uomini, e tutti abbraccia
con vero amor, porgendo
valida e pronta ed aspettando aita
negli alterni perigli e nelle angosce
della guerra comune. Ed alle offese
dell'uomo armar la destra, e laccio porre
al vicino ed inciampo,
stolto crede così qual fôra in campo
cinto d'oste contraria, in sul più vivo
incalzar degli assalti,
gl'inimici obbliando, acerbe gare
imprender con gli amici,
e sparger fuga e fulminar col brando
infra i propri guerrieri.
Così fatti pensieri
quando fien, come fûr, palesi al volgo,
e quell'orror che primo
contra l'empia natura
strinse i mortali in social catena,
fia ricondotto in parte
da verace saper, l'onesto e il retto
conversar cittadino,
e giustizia e pietade, altra radice
avranno allor che non superbe fole,
ove fondata probità del volgo
così star suole in piede
quale star può quel ch'ha in error la sede.

Sovente in queste rive,
che, desolate, a bruno

himself both brave and strong, not adding hate
or anger with his brother,
the heaviest cross of all,
to natural misery, and he never blames
man for his troubles, but applies the guilt
to the real culprit, nature, who is mother
to us in fact, but stepmother in feeling.
He calls her enemy; and considering,
which is the truth, that human
society was first composed and trained
against this enemy,
he sees all men as allies with each other
and he embraces all
with real love, and offers
powerful and ready aid, expecting help
in turn as pain and danger come and go
in this shared war. And arming to attack
one's fellow man, or setting stumbling-blocks
and snares against one's neighbour
seems stupid, as upon a battlefield
ringed by a hostile army, at the highest
pressure of the assault,
to forget the enemy and pick a bitter
fight with your loving friends,
and spreading panic, flash your lightning sword
among your own side's men.
When thoughts like this again
circulate in the street as they did once,
and that original terror
which first bound men together
in social chains against iniquitous nature,
has been brought back, in part,
by knowledge of the truth – then the fair dealing
of upright citizens,
justice and piety, will have other roots
than fables, fibs, and fancies of proud man
on which the established ethics of the crowd
stands now – if it does stand
on such false footing, on such shifting sand.

Often on these deserted
banks, which the hardening flow

veste il flutto indurato, e par che ondeggi,
seggo la notte; e su la mesta landa
in purissimo azzurro
veggo dall'alto fiammeggiar le stelle,
cui di lontan fa specchio
il mare, e tutto di scintille in giro
per lo vòto seren brillare il mondo.
E poi che gli occhi a quelle luci appunto,
ch'a lor sembrano un punto,
e sono immense, in guisa
che un punto a petto a lor son terra e mare
veracemente; a cui
l'uomo non pur, ma questo
globo ove l'uomo è nulla,
sconosciuto è del tutto; e quando miro
quegli ancor più senz'alcun fin remoti
nodi quasi di stelle
ch'a noi paion qual nebbia, a cui non l'uomo
e non la terra sol, ma tutte in uno,
del numero infinite e della mole,
con l'aureo sole insiem, le nostre stelle
o sono ignote, o così paion come
essi alla terra, un punto
di luce nebulosa; al pensier mio
che sembri allora, o prole
dell'uomo? E rimembrando
il tuo stato quaggiù, di cui fa segno
il suol ch'io premo; e poi dall'altra parte,
che te signora e fine
credi tu data al Tutto, e quante volte
favoleggiar ti piacque, in questo oscuro
granel di sabbia, il qual di terra ha nome,
per tua cagion, dell'universe cose
scender gli autori, e conversar sovente
co' tuoi piacevolmente, e che i derisi
sogni rinnovellando, ai saggi insulta
fin la presente età, che in conoscenza
ed in civil costume
sembra tutte avanzar; qual moto allora,
mortal prole infelice, o qual pensiero
verso te finalmente il cor m'assale?
Non so se il riso o la pietà prevale.

has dressed in brown, like slow arrested waves,
I sit at night; and from this sad expanse
in the pure blue above
I see the distant flaming of the stars,
to which the far-off sea is
a mirror, the whole world a brilliant wheel
of sparks across the cloudless emptiness.
And when I point my eyes toward these lights
which seem mere points to them –
yet they're so big the earth
and sea beside them are themselves a point
in real size, and to them
mankind and all this round
planet where man is nothing
are undiscovered still – and when I stare
at those yet further, endlessly far off
as it were knots of stars,
which blur like mist to us – from which not only
man and the earth but all the stars we see
together with the golden sun, our stars,
infinite both in number and in mass,
are quite unknown, or else appear as they
are seen from earth, a point
of cloudy light – where on my scale of thought
do you show then, o child
of man? And reckoning up
your status here below, to which this ground
I tread bears witness; that in spite of this
you can believe yourself
given as lord and purpose to the Cosmos,
and that you always loved inventing stories,
of how, on this obscure worn grain of sand
called Terra, the founders of the universe
came down on your account and often talked
to you and yours with pleasure; and that this age,
even this present age, which seems in knowledge
and public manners better than all others,
can still insult the wise
by breathing life in these deflated dreams –
what feelings then, unhappy mortal kind,
what thoughts attack me when we meet? – a burst
of pity, or laughter? I don't know which comes first.

Come d'arbor cadendo un picciol pomo,
cui là nel tardo autunno
maturità senz'altra forza atterra,
d'un popol di formiche i dolci alberghi,
cavati in molle gleba
con gran lavoro, e l'opre
e le ricchezze che adunate a prova
con lungo affaticar l'assidua gente
avea provvidamente al tempo estivo,
schiaccia, diserta e copre
in un punto; così d'alto piombando,
dall'utero tonante
scagliata al ciel profondo,
di ceneri e di pomici e di sassi
notte e ruina, infusa
di bollenti ruscelli,
o pel montano fianco
furiosa tra l'erba
di liquefatti massi
e di metalli e d'infocata arena
scendendo immensa piena,
le cittadi che il mar là su l'estremo
lido aspergea, confuse
e infranse e ricoperse
in pochi istanti: onde su quelle or pasce
la capra, e città nove
sorgon dall'altra banda, a cui sgabello
son le sepolte, e le prostrate mura
l'arduo monte al suo piè quasi calpesta.
Non ha natura al seme
dell'uom più stima o cura
che alla formica: e se più rara in quello
che nell'altra è la strage,
non avvien ciò d'altronde
fuor che l'uom sue prosapie ha men feconde.

Ben mille ed ottocento
anni varcâr poi che sparîro, oppressi
dall'ignea forza, i popolati seggi,
e il villanello intento
ai vigneti, che a stento in questi campi
nutre la morta zolla e incenerita,

As when a little apple from its tree
starts falling, brought to earth
in the late autumn by no other force
than ripeness; and a tribe of ants, their sweet
safe homes dug in soft soil
laboriously, their works
and riches that, competing in long toil,
their persevering species had assembled
with forethought in the earlier summery time,
are squashed, laid waste, and covered
in a single second; so, dropping from a height,
out of that thundering womb
shot deeply into heaven,
darkness and ruin made of ash and pumice
and boulders, either fused
in little boiling streams
or down the mountain's side
sliding through grass in fury,
immense and overflowing
with solids turned to liquid, running metals,
and sands of pouring fire,
fell on the cities that the sea once used
to sprinkle with its edges,
ground them together, smashed them,
and covered them in moments: now above them
goats browse, while there new cities
rise on the other side, using as footstools
the buried ones, and the steep mountain almost
tramples the old walls prostrate at its foot.
For nature does not honour
or nurse the seed of man
more than the ant's; and if destruction strikes
less often us than them,
there is one explanation:
man is less fruitful in his generation.

A thousand and eight hundred
years have gone by since, crushed by fiery force,
those swarming nests of people disappeared;
and still the peasant busy
about his vines which in these fields the dead
incinerated soil can scarcely nourish,

ancor leva lo sguardo
sospettoso alla vetta
fatal, che nulla mai fatta più mite
ancor siede tremenda, ancor minaccia
a lui strage ed ai figli ed agli averi
lor poverelli. E spesso
il meschino in sul tetto
dell'ostel villereccio, alla vagante
aura giacendo tutta notte insonne
e balzando più volte, esplora il corso
del temuto bollor, che si riversa
dall'inesausto grembo
su l'arenoso dorso, a cui riluce
di Capri la marina
e di Napoli il porto e Mergellina.
E se appressar lo vede, o se nel cupo
del domestico pozzo ode mai l'acqua
fervendo gorgogliar, desta i figliuoli,
desta la moglie in fretta, e via, con quanto
di lor cose rapir posson, fuggendo,
vede lontan l'usato
suo nido, e il picciol campo,
che gli fu dalla fame unico schermo,
preda al flutto rovente,
che crepitando giunge, e inesorato
durabilmente sovra quei si spiega.
Torna al celeste raggio
dopo l'antica obblivion l'estinta
Pompei, come sepolto
scheletro, cui di terra
avarizia o pietà rende all'aperto;
e dal deserto foro
diritto infra le file
dei mozzi colonnati il peregrino
lunge contempla il bipartito giogo
e la cresta fumante,
che alla sparsa ruina ancor minaccia.
E nell'orror della secreta notte
per li vacui teatri,
per li templi deformi e per le rotte
case, ove i parti il pipistrello asconde,
come sinistra face

lifts even now suspicious
eyes to the fatal peak
which not at all the milder sits above him
still to be feared, still threatening on his head
and on his children and their poor possessions
the loss of all. And often
this wretch, who on the roof
of his rustic house lies sleepless all night long
in the wandering airs, starts up and several times
checks the direction of the fearful flow
of steaming, bubbling stuff that is poured down
from that untiring lap
over the sandy flanks, reflecting light
back from the shores of Capri,
from Naples harbour and from Mergellina.
And if he sees it's closer, if he hears
the water stir in his domestic well
and gurgle, then he wakes his little children,
rushes and wakes his wife, and off, in flight,
with all the things of theirs they can snatch up,
sees from far off the familiar
nest and its little field,
the only shield he had against their starving,
fall to the red-hot tide
that crackles as it comes and spreads itself
over them, hardening and immune to prayers.
Back to the rays of heaven
after antique oblivion comes extinguished
Pompei, like a buried
skeleton which the greed
for land, or piety, brings again to the surface;
and from the abandoned forum
upright between the ranks
of chopped-off colonnades the traveller catches
a distant view of the divided summit
and of the smoking ridge
still threatening the scattered ruins below.
And in the prickling fear of lonely night
over the empty theatres,
over the sagging temples and the broken
houses where bats conceal their new-born young,
like an ill-omened lamp

che per vòti palagi atra s'aggiri,
corre il baglior della funerea lava,
che di lontan per l'ombre
rosseggia e i lochi intorno intorno tinge.
Così, dell'uomo ignara e dell'etadi
ch'ei chiama antiche, e del seguir che fanno
dopo gli avi i nepoti,
sta natura ognor verde, anzi procede
per sì lungo cammino
che sembra star. Caggiono i regni intanto,
passan genti e linguaggi: ella nol vede:
e l'uom d'eternità s'arroga il vanto.

E tu, lenta ginestra,
che di selve odorate
queste campagne dispogliate adorni,
anche tu presto alla crudel possanza
soccomberai del sotterraneo foco,
che ritornando al loco
già noto, stenderà l'avaro lembo
su tue molli foreste. E piegherai
sotto il fascio mortal non renitente
il tuo capo innocente:
ma non piegato insino allora indarno
codardamente supplicando innanzi
al futuro oppressor; ma non eretto
con forsennato orgoglio inver le stelle,
né sul deserto, dove
e la sede e i natali
non per voler ma per fortuna avesti;
ma più saggia, ma tanto
meno inferma dell'uom, quanto le frali
tue stirpi non credesti
o dal fato o da te fatte immortali.

GIACOMO LEOPARDI

that whirls darkly through empty rooms of palaces,
the glimmer runs, from that funereal lava
that glows across the shadows
a far-off red that tints the places round.
So, unconscious of man and of the ages
that he calls ancient, and the path the children
follow the parents down,
Nature is always green, or rather she
goes such a long slow walk
she seems unmoving. Meanwhile empires fall,
peoples and languages die – she doesn't see –
and arrogant man is claiming he's eternal.

And you, resilient broom,
who with your perfumed bushes
adorn this stripped and ravaged countryside,
you too will soon succumb before the cruel
power of this fire that rises underground
and coming back to places
already known will spread its greedy fringes
on your soft forests. And you without resisting
will bow your innocent and yielding head
under the killing burden:
but not till then bowing it, like a coward,
in unsuccessful pleas before the face
of your determined conqueror: nor raising
that head with frantic pride towards the stars
or else against the desert
where you were set and born
not by your wish, but by blind fortune's hand;
yet wiser, and so much
less weak than man, you never
thought your frail shoots were planned
by fate or by yourself to live for ever.

GIACOMO LEOPARDI

Sant' Ambrogio

Vostra Eccellenza che mi sta in cagnesco
per que' pochi scherzucci di dozzina,
e mi gabella per anti-tedesco
perché metto le birbe alla berlina;
o senta il caso avvenuto di fresco
a me che girellando una mattina,
càpito in Sant'Ambrogio di Milano,
in quello vecchio, là fuori di mano.

M'era compagno il figlio giovinetto
d'un di que' capi un po' pericolosi,
di quel tal Sandro, autor d'un romanzetto
ove si tratta di promessi sposi...
Che fa il nesci, Eccellenza? o non l'ha letto?
Ah, intendo: il suo cervel, Dio lo riposi,
in tutt'altre faccende affaccendato,
a questa roba è morto e sotterrato.

Entro; e ti trovo un pieno di soldati,
di que' soldati settentrïonali
come sarebbe Boemi e Croati,
messi qui nella vigna a far da pali:
difatto, se ne stavano impalati,
come sogliono in faccia a' generali,
co' baffi di capecchio e con que' musi,
davanti a Dio diritti come fusi.

Mi tenni indietro; ché piovuto in mezzo
di quella maramaglia, io non le nego
d'aver provato un senso di ribrezzo
che lei non prova in grazia dell'impiego.
Sentiva un'afa, un alito di lezzo:
scusi, Eccellenza, mi parean di sego
in quella bella casa del Signore
fin le candele dell'altar maggiore.

St Ambrose's

Your Excellency, though you snarl and growl
At me for making up a few poor jokes,
And call me anti-German, with a scowl,
Because I pillory some political crooks,
Just hear what happened to me on a stroll
The other morning, rising with the larks,
When on the edge of town I came across
The old basilica there, you know, St Ambrose'.

For company, I had the young son of a l-
iberal – his father has a 'dangerous head',
Manzoni, author of a romantic novel
About some people promising to wed.
Oh sir! Don't say that doesn't ring a bell!
Not read it? Oh, I see – your brain is dead
(God give it rest!) and buried to such stuff –
Being already occupied enough.

Well, I go in and find the military class
Have crammed it full, some of your northern pals,
Croatians and Bohemians is my guess –
Stuck here among our vines like vineyard poles –
In fact they stand with ramrods up their arse
The way they do when facing generals,
Wooden-faced men like spindles with their flax
Moustaches to be spun as God inspects.

I kept well back, for falling in the midst
Of that vile rabble, I will not conceal
I suffered such a shudder of disgust
As you, thanks to your job, no longer feel.
Their stinking breath produced a muggy blast
That – pardon me, Your Honour – made me smell
Suet all through God's house: I even caught a
Whiff from the candles on the highest altar.

Ma in quella che s'appresta il sacerdote
a consacrar la mistica vivanda,
di subita dolcezza mi percuote
su, di verso l'altare, un suon di banda.
Dalle trombe di guerra uscìan le note
come di voce che si raccomanda,
d'una gente che gema in duri stenti
e de' perduti beni si rammenti.

Era un coro del Verdi; il coro a Dio
là de' Lombardi miseri assetati;
quello, *O Signore, dal tetto natio,*
che tanti petti ha scossi e inebrïati.
Qui cominciai a non esser più io;
e come se que' così doventati
fossero gente della nostra gente,
entrai nel branco involontariamente.

Che vuol ella, Eccellenza, il pezzo è bello,
poi nostro, e poi suonato come va;
e coll'arte di mezzo, e col cervello
dato all'arte, l'ubbie si buttan là.
Ma cessato che fu, dentro, bel bello
io ritornava a star come la sa:
quand'eccoti per farmi un altro tiro,
da quelle bocche che parean di ghiro

un cantico tedesco lento lento
per l'äer sacro a Dio mosse le penne.
Era preghiera, e mi parea lamento,
d'un suono grave flebile solenne,
tal che sempre nell'anima lo sento:
e mi stupisco che in quelle cotenne,
in que' fantocci esotici di legno,
potesse l'armonia fino a quel segno.

Sentìa nell'inno la dolcezza amara
de' canti uditi da fanciullo: il core
che da voce domestica gl'impara
ce li ripete i giorni del dolore:
un pensier mesto della madre cara,
un desiderio di pace e d'amore,
uno sgomento di lontano esilio,
che mi faceva andare in visibilio.

But at the moment when the priest prepares
To consecrate the theological food,
A sudden sweetness struck me, musical airs
From somewhere near the altar and the rood,
Notes from the trumpets of these warriors
Like voices pleading to be understood,
People in want so dire they only groan
And meekly miss the goods they used to own.

It was a Verdi chorus, the one addressed
To God by Lombards thirsty on crusade –
'Lord, from the house where we were born and raised' –
Which has made drunk so many a heart and head.
Here I lost all the self I once possessed
And just as if these so-and-sos were made
Blood of our blood and stood in our position,
I joined the mob of them without volition.

You see, Your Honour, the piece is very fine,
It's one of ours, they played it the right way –
With art as go-between and in a mind
Given to art, prejudice drops away.
But as soon as it was over, my inside
Started to feel the same old nausea –
When suddenly, to throw me once again,
Out of the mouse-mouths of those whiskery men

Into the air of God with very slow
Heaven-bound wingbeats flew a German anthem:
It was a prayer, but seemed a song of sorrow
It was so heavy, full of tears, and solemn –
Still I can hear it sounding in my soul,
And still I marvel that in men like them,
Those life-sized puppets carved of foreign wood,
There could be harmony that sounds so good.

I tasted in that hymn the bitter sweetness
Of songs first heard in childhood, ones the brain
That learned them from beloved household voices
Repeats instinctively on days of pain:
A sad reminder of our darling mothers,
A longing to have peace and love again,
A horror at our distant banishment –
I was in ecstasies of sentiment.

E quando tacque mi lasciò pensoso
di pensieri più forti e più soavi.
«Costor,» dicea tra me «Re pauroso
degl'italici moti e degli slavi
strappa a' lor tetti, e qua senza riposo
schiavi gli spinge per tenerci schiavi;
gli spinge di Croazia e di Boemme,
come mandre a svernar nelle maremme.

A dura vita, a dura disciplina,
muti, derisi, solitari stanno,
strumenti ciechi d'occhiuta rapina
che lor non tocca e che forse non sanno;
e quest'odio, che mai non avvicina
il popolo lombardo all'alemanno,
giova a chi regna dividendo, e teme
popoli avversi affratellati insieme.

Povera gente! lontana da' suoi,
in un paese qui che le vuol male,
chi sa che in fondo all'anima po' poi
non mandi a quel paese il principale:
gioco che l'hanno in tasca come noi».
Qui, se non fuggo, abbraccio un caporale,
colla su' brava mazza di nocciuolo,
duro e piantato lì come un piolo.

GIUSEPPE GIUSTI
(1809-1850)

And when the silence fell, I was left thinking
Much kinder thoughts – I also felt quite brave.
I told myself, 'That king's afraid, expecting
Revolts in Italy and among the Slavs,
So he's snatched them from their homes, and sent them reeling
Straight here, as slaves to keep down other slaves,
Driving them down from Croatia and Bohemia
Like sheep to winter in the low Maremma.

Under this terrible life and discipline
They stand there speechless, laughed at and alone,
Blind instruments of a sharp-eyed robber chieftain,
Getting no share, not knowing what they've done.
This hatred that has always kept us foreign,
Not neighbours, Lombard hating Allamann,
This serves the king – divide and rule – who fears
His peoples might turn round and see they're brothers.

Poor creatures, far from everyone they know,
Stuck among people who must wish them ill,
Who knows if from the bottom of their soul
They sometimes curse the emperor to hell!
I bet they loathe him just as much as we do.
Here, I'd to leave, or I'd have kissed a corporal
Who rooted there firm as a fence-post stood
Twirling his swagger-stick of hazel-wood.

GIUSEPPE GIUSTI

Dinanzi alle terme di Caracalla

Corron tra 'l Celio fosche e l'Aventino
le nubi: il vento dal pian tristo move
umido: in fondo stanno i monti albani
bianchi di neve.

A le cineree trecce alzato il velo
verde, nel libro una britanna cerca
queste minacce di romane mura
al cielo e al tempo.

Continui, densi, neri, crocidanti
versansi i corvi come fluttuando
contro i due muri ch'a più ardua sfida
levansi enormi.

«Vecchi giganti, – par che insista irato
l'augure stormo – a che tentate il cielo?»
Grave per l'aure vien da Laterano
suon di campane.

Ed un ciociaro, nel mantello avvolto,
grave fischiando tra la folta barba,
passa e non guarda. Febbre, io qui t'invoco,
nume presente.

Se ti fûr cari i grandi occhi piangenti
e de le madri le protese braccia
te deprecanti, o dea, dal reclinato
capo dei figli:

se ti fu cara su 'l Palazio eccelso
l'ara vetusta (ancor lambiva il Tebro
l'evandrio colle, e veleggiando a sera
tra 'l Campidoglio

e l'Aventino il reduce quirite
guardava in alto la città quadrata
dal sole arrisa, e mormorava un lento
saturnio carme);

Facing the Baths of Caracalla

Dull between the Aventine and the Caelian
clouds are running: wind from the evil plain blows
damp: the Alban Hills in the background stand out
white from a snowfall.

With her green veil raised on her ashy tresses
in the book a lady from Britain looks up
what these Roman walls can be named, that challenge
heaven and time, both.

Thick and fast, continuous, black, all croaking,
crows come pouring in like an endless breaker
onto these two walls, of a monstrous height and
threatening higher.

'Ancient giants,' cry the prophetic birds, or
seem to, harshly, 'why are you trying heaven?'
Heavy down the breeze there arrives a sound of
bells from the Lateran.

And a peasant, pulling his cloak tight about him,
passes, whistling deep in his bass's thick beard,
never looking up. I invoke you, Fever,
god always present:

If you ever loved the wide-open weeping
eyes of mothers and their imploring narrow
arms that beg you, goddess, to leave the lolling
heads of their children –

If you once were pleased by your ancient altar
on the Palatine, when the Tiber still licked
at Evander's hill-town and, sailing home at
sunset between those

hills, the Capitol and the Aventine, the early
civis could look up at Quadrata Roma
smiled on by the sun, as he slowly hummed a
song in Saturnians –

Febbre, m'ascolta. Gli uomini novelli
quinci respingi e lor picciole cose:
religïoso è questo orror: la dea
Roma qui dorme.

Poggiata il capo al Palatino augusto,
tra 'l Celio aperte e l'Aventin le braccia,
per la Capena i forti omeri stende
a l'Appia via.

GIOSUÈ CARDUCCI
(1835-1907)

Fever, hear my prayers: Dislodge today's men,
and their small possessions, from this whole precinct.
It's religious fear I express: the goddess
Rome is asleep here.

With the noble Palatine for a pillow,
arms wrapped round the Aventine and the Caelian,
through Capena down to the Appian Way she
spreads her strong torso.

GIOSUÈ CARDUCCI

Davanti il Castel Vecchio di Verona

Tal mormoravi possente e rapido
sotto i romani ponti, o verde Adige,
brillando dal limpido gorgo,
la tua scorrente canzone al sole,

quando Odoacre dinanzi a l'impeto
di Teodorico cesse, e tra l'èrulo
eccidio passavan su i carri
diritte e bionde le donne amàle

entro la bella Verona, odinici
carmi intonando: raccolta al vescovo
intorno, l'italica plebe
sporgea la croce supplice a' Goti.

Tale da i monti di neve rigidi,
ne la diffusa letizia argentea
del placido verno, o fuggente
infaticato, mormori e vai

sotto il merlato ponte scaligero,
tra nere moli, tra squallidi alberi,
a i colli sereni, a le torri,
onde abbrunate piangon le insegne

il ritornante giorno funereo
del primo eletto re da l'Italia
francata: tu, Adige, canti
la tua scorrente canzone al sole.

Anch'io, bel fiume, canto: e il mio cantico
nel picciol verso raccoglie i secoli,
e il cuore al pensiero balzando
segue la strofe che sorge e trema.

Ma la mia strofe vanirà torbida
ne gli anni: eterno poeta, o Adige,
tu ancor tra le sparse macerie
di questi colli turriti, quando

In front of the Old Castle at Verona

You made this murmur, rapid and powerful,
under the Roman bridges, green Adige,
sparkling in bright transparent eddies,
this was the anthem you poured out sunwards

when Odoacer, facing Theodoric's
onslaught, gave way and through the Herulian
dead went the chariots bearing those blonde
straight-backed Amalian women into

this fair Verona, chanting their war-songs in
honour of Odin: gathering close to their
bishop, the poor Italian people
held out the cross to the Goths and pleaded.

Even from mountains frozen and stiff with snow,
during the spread-out silvery happiness
of peaceful winter, tireless runner,
still you are murmuring and diving under

the crenellated bridge of the Scaligers,
between black buildings, under the dismal trees,
towards clear hill-tops, and by towers whose
family standards hang down in mourning

dark for the funeral day coming back again
of our first chosen king of all Italy
in freedom; Adige, you're singing
still to the sun the same flowing anthem.

I too, fair river, sing and my canticle
gathers in these small verses the centuries,
while, leaping up with thought, the heart-beat
follows the rising and trembling stanza.

But through the years my stanza will vanish in
the dust: while you, forever possessed by song,
still flowing through the rubble scattered
over these towerless hills in times when

su le rovine de la basilica
di Zeno al sole sibili il còlubro,
ancor canterai nel deserto,
i tedi insonni de l'infinito.

Giosuè Carducci

here in the wreck of Zeno's basilica
there will be just snakes hissing towards the sun,
still in that waste land, Adige, you shall
sing of eternity's sleepless boredom.

GIOSUÈ CARDUCCI

Alle fonti del Clitumno

Ancor dal monte, che di foschi ondeggia
frassini al vento mormoranti e lunge
per l'aure odora fresco di silvestri
salvie e di timi,

scendon nel vespero umido, o Clitumno,
a te le greggi: a te l'umbro fanciullo
la riluttante pecora ne l'onda
immerge, mentre

vèr' lui dal seno de la madre adusta,
che scalza siede al casolare e canta,
una poppante volgesi e dal viso
tondo sorride:

pensoso il padre, di caprine pelli
l'anche ravvolto come i fauni antichi,
regge il dipinto plaustro e la forza
de' bei giovenchi,

de' bei giovenchi dal quadrato petto,
erti su 'l capo le lunate corna,
dolci ne gli occhi, nivëi, che il mite
Virgilio amava.

Oscure intanto fumano le nubi
su l'Apennino: grande, austera, verde
da le montagne digradanti in cerchio
l'Umbrïa guarda.

Salve, Umbria verde, e tu del puro fonte
nume Clitumno! Sento in cuor l'antica
patria e aleggiarmi su l'accesa fronte
gl'itali iddii.

Chi l'ombre indusse del piangente salcio
su' rivi sacri? ti rapisca il vento
de l'Apennino, o molle pianta, amore
d'umili tempi!

At the Springs of the Clitumnus

Even today from the hill, whose back ripples
with dim ash trees muttering in the wind and
spreads far on the breeze wafts of its own fresh smell
of wild sage and thyme,

the flocks come down through moistening air at sunset
to you, Clitumnus; still the Umbrian boy
plunges his struggling animal under your
ruffled surface, while

to see him from the breast of their tanned mother
who sits barefoot beside the shieling and sings,
his small unweaned sister pushes round and sends
a full round-faced smile;

there still the anxious father, with his thighs wrapped
in hairy goatskins like the fauns long ago,
rules and directs his painted cart and the strength
of his fine oxen,

those lovely oxen with their square honest chests,
and crescent horns set high above their foreheads,
and great soft eyes, the snowy beasts that tender
Virgil was fond of.

Dark as smoke all this time the clouds are rising
over the Apennines. Great and bare and green,
down from the rings of ever paler mountains,
Umbria looks on.

I greet green Umbria, I greet the numen
of the pure spring Clitumnus! The old land beats
in my heart: I feel pre-Roman gods flutter
at my burning brow.

Who brought the shadows of the weeping willow
to these sacred banks? May the Apennine wind
carry you off, soft plant, bending favourite
of decadent times!

Qui pugni a' verni e arcane istorie frema
co 'l palpitante maggio ilice nera,
a cui d'allegra giovinezza il tronco
l'edera veste:

qui folti a torno l'emergente nume
stieno, giganti vigili, i cipressi;
e tu fra l'ombre, tu fatali canta
carmi, o Clitumno.

O testimone di tre imperi, dinne
come il grave umbro ne' duelli atroce
cesse a l'astato velite e la forte
Etruria crebbe:

di' come sovra le congiunte ville
dal superato Cimino a gran passi
calò Gradivo poi, piantando i segni
fieri di Roma.

Ma tu placavi, indigete comune
italo nume, i vincitori a i vinti,
e, quando tonò il punico furore
dal Trasimeno,

per gli antri tuoi salì grido, e la torta
lo ripercosse buccina da i monti:
– O tu che pasci i buoi presso Mevania
caliginosa,

e tu che i proni colli ari a la sponda
del Nar sinistra, e tu che i boschi abbatti
sovra Spoleto verdi o ne la marzia
Todi fai nozze,

lascia il bue grasso tra le canne, lascia
il torel fulvo a mezzo solco, lascia
ne l'inclinata quercia il cuneo, lascia
la sposa a l'ara;

e corri, corri, corri! con la scure
corri e co' dardi, con la clava e l'asta:
corri! minaccia gl'itali penati
Ànnibal diro. –

Here black ilex should stand to fight the winter
storms, and in pulsing May tell forgotten tales,
shivering, with ivy on its trunk to clothe it
in youth and gladness.

Here, set thick round the emerging water-god,
cypresses should be standing, giant guardsmen;
and you, Clitumnus, in their shadows, sing us
our fated epics.

O witness of three empires, tell the stories:
how the heavy Umbrian fierce in battles
gave in to light-armed men with lances, and strong
Etruria grew;

how next over the confederated towns,
crossing Monte Cimino in great strides, Mars,
the Roman god of marching, swooped and planted
his savage banners.

But you, their native common god, Italian,
made peace between the victors and the vanquished,
and, when the Carthaginian fury thundered
at Lake Trasimene,

a cry was heard to rise from your caves, echoed
by the twisted battle-trumpet through the hills:
'O you who take your oxen to the fields near
foggy Bevagna,

and you who plough the gentle slopes on the left
bank of the Nar, who fell the trees green above
Spoleto or who in Mars's town, Todi,
walk to your wedding,

leave the fat ox among the reed-beds, leave the
brown bullock halfway down the furrow, leave the
wedge in the already leaning oak, leave the
bride at the altar –

and run, run; run with the swing of your axes
and hunting-spears, run with your clubs and lances:
Cruel Hannibal threatens every household
god in Italy.'

Deh come rise d'alma luce il sole
per questa chiostra di bei monti, quando
urlanti vide e ruinanti in fuga
l'alta Spoleto

i Mauri immani e i nùmidi cavalli
con mischia oscena, e, sovra loro, nembi
di ferro, flutti d'olio ardente, e i canti
de la vittoria!

Tutto ora tace. Nel sereno gorgo
la tenue miro salïente vena:
trema, e d'un lieve pullular lo specchio
segna de l'acque.

Ride sepolta a l'imo una foresta
breve, e rameggia immobile: il diaspro
par che si mischi in flessuosi amori
con l'ametista,

e di zaffiro i fior paiono, ed hanno
de l'adamante rigido i riflessi,
e splendon freddi e chiamano ai silenzi
del verde fondo.

A piè de i monti e de le querce a l'ombra
co' fiumi, o Italia, è de' tuoi carmi il fonte.
Visser le ninfe, vissero: e un divino
talamo è questo.

Emergean lunghe ne' fluenti veli
naiadi azzurre, e per la cheta sera
chiamavan alto le sorelle brune
da le montagne,

e danze sotto l'imminente luna
guidavan, liete ricantando in coro
di Giano eterno e quanto amor lo vinse
di Camesena.

Egli dal cielo, autoctona virago
ella: fu letto l'Apennin fumante:
velaro i nembi il grande amplesso, e nacque
l'itala gente.

Oh how the sun glowed with kindly light over
this cloister of lovely mountains on that day
when from its height Spoleto saw howling and
falling as they fled

the monstrous Moors and the Numidian horsemen
horribly mixed together, and above them
showers of steel, a tide of burning oil and
chants of victory!

Everything's silent now. In the cloudless pool
I watch a delicate vein of liquid rise:
it trembles and with a light pulse disturbs the
mirroring surface.

Buried right at the bottom lies a small wood
shining and branching without motion: jasper
appears to blend with amethyst in supple
loving manoeuvres;

the flowers of sapphire seem to be coming out –
they have reflections like unbending diamond;
coldly they burn and summon to the silence
of the pool's green floor.

At the feet of mountains, in the shade of oaks,
Italy's poems, like her streams, take their rise.
There were nymphs once: they did live; this place has been
a bedroom for gods.

They came out, tall, in streaming veils of water,
sky-blue naiads, and pierced the quiet evening
with loud calls to their brown sisters to join them
out of the mountains,

and, under the hovering moon, formed figures
of dances as a chorus gladly singing
about immortal Janus and how much he
loved Camesena.

He from the sky, she a heroic girl from
this soil; the cloud-banked Apennine was their bed;
cloud-bursts curtained the great embrace, the birth of
Italy's people.

Tutto ora tace, o vedovo Clitumno,
tutto: de' vaghi tuoi delùbri un solo
t'avanza, e dentro pretestato nume
tu non vi siedi.

Non più perfusi del tuo fiume sacro
menano i tori, vittime orgogliose,
trofei romani a i templi aviti: Roma
più non trionfa.

Più non trionfa, poi che un galileo
di rosse chiome il Campidoglio ascese,
gittolle in braccio una sua croce, e disse
– Portala, e servi. –

Fuggîr le ninfe a piangere ne' fiumi
occulte e dentro i cortici materni,
od ululando dileguaron come
nuvole a i monti

quando una strana compagnia, tra i bianchi
templi spogliati e i colonnati infranti,
procedé lenta, in neri sacchi avvolta,
litanïando,

e sovra i campi del lavoro umano
sonanti e i clivi memori d'impero
fece deserto, et il deserto disse
regno di Dio.

Strappâr le turbe a i santi aratri, a i vecchi
padri aspettanti, a le fiorenti mogli;
ovunque il divo sol benedicea,
maledicenti.

Maledicenti a l'opre de la vita
e de l'amore, ei deliraro atroci
congiugnimenti di dolor con Dio
su rupi e in grotte:

discesero ebri di dissolvimento
a le cittadi, e in ridde paurose
al crocefisso supplicarono, empi,
d'essere abietti.

Everything's silent, Clitumnus: you live on
abandoned; of your elegant shrines just one
is left you and you don't recline inside it,
god in a toga.

No more are bulls, sprinkled from your sacred stream,
victims proud to be sacrificed, made to pull
Roman trophies to our grandfathers' temples:
Rome has no triumphs,

not any longer, since a Galilean
with red hair climbed the steps of her Capitol,
threw in her arms one of his crosses, and said:
'Carry that; serve me.'

The nymphs fled to weep hidden among their streams
or in the bark of trees that once had borne them,
or with a wail of sorrow vanished in air
like the clouds on hills,

when a strange foreign company, through the white
denuded temples and broken colonnades
came in slow procession, wrapped in black sackcloth,
chanting litanies,

and on those fields, that Campus resonant still
with human action, and those imperial hills,
imposed a desert and then called that desert
the kingdom of God.

They tore men from the holy work of ploughing,
the hopes of their old fathers, their flowering wives:
wherever the godlike sun threw a blessing,
they came with a curse.

And putting curses on every act of life
and natural love, they raved about inhuman
ways of joining pain and their God together
among rocks and caves:

then they descended, drunk with self-destruction,
on the cities: in dreadful whirling dances
praying (sacrilege!) to that crucified man
to make them abject.

Salve, o serena de l'Ilisso in riva,
o intera e dritta a i lidi almi del Tebro
anima umana; i foschi dì passaro,
risorgi e regna.

E tu, pia madre di giovenchi invitti
a franger glebe e rintegrar maggesi,
e d'annitrenti in guerra aspri polledri
Italia madre,

madre di biade e viti e leggi eterne
ed inclite arti a raddolcir la vita,
salve! a te i canti de l'antica lode
io rinnovello.

Plaudono i monti al carme e i boschi e l'acque
de l'Umbria verde: in faccia a noi fumando
ed anelando nuove industrie in corsa
fischia il vapore.

[Roma, 9 ottobre 1881]

GIOSUÈ CARDUCCI

I greet you, soul of man, serene from Athens'
rivers or straight and healthy from the Tiber's
nourishing banks: the dark time is over: rise
again and govern.

And you, fond mother of oxen unbeaten
at breaking soil or opening the fallow,
also of fiery colts neighing for battle,
mother Italy,

bearing blades of corn and vines, eternal law
and famous arts that make our lives sweet again,
I greet you too; for you I sing again now
the ancient praise-songs.

The praise is echoed by the hills, woods, waters
of green Umbria: opposite us, steaming,
and panting to put new industries in train,
an engine whistles.

[Rome, 9 October 1881]

GIOSUÈ CARDUCCI

Cavallino

O bel clivo fiorito Cavallino
ch'io varcai co' leggiadri eguali a schiera
al mio bel tempo; chi sa dir se l'era
d'olmo la tua parlante ombra o di pino?

Era busso ricciuto o biancospino,
da cui dorata trasparia la sera?
C'è un campanile tra una selva nera,
che canta, bianco, l'inno mattutino?

Non so: ché quando a te s'appressa il vano
desìo, per entro il cielo fuggitivo
te vedo incerta visïon fluire.

So ch'or sembri il paese allor lontano
lontano, che dal tuo fiorito clivo
io rimirai nel limpido avvenire.

GIOVANNI PASCOLI
(1855-1912)
'Ricordi' IX

Cavallino

O lovely flowery hill, dear Cavallino,
I climbed you with my pretty friends, together
in our lovely days of youth: who can say whether
your talking shadows were of elm or pine?

Was it a hawthorn that let through the rays
of evening, gilding them, or a dense box-tree?
Is there a dark wood there around a belfry
all white, that sings the hymns of morning praise?

I cannot say: for when my vain desire
comes near you, you flow off uncertainly
into the sky, a vision I can't capture.

I do know you seem now to be that country,
so distant then, I gazed toward with awe
from your flowery side, down in the limpid future.

GIOVANNI PASCOLI
'Memories' IX, from *Myricae*

117

Patria

Sogno d'un dì d'estate.

Quanto scampanellare
tremulo di cicale!
Stridule pel filare
moveva il maestrale
le foglie accartocciate.

Scendea tra gli olmi il sole
in fascie polverose;
erano in ciel due sole
nuvole, tenui, róse:
due bianche spennellate

in tutto il ciel turchino.

Siepi di melograno,
fratte di tamerice,
il palpito lontano
d'una trebbïatrice,
l'angelus argentino...

dov'ero? Le campane
mi dissero dov'ero,
piangendo, mentre un cane
latrava al forestiero,
che andava a capo chino.

GIOVANNI PASCOLI
'Dall' alba al tramonto' VII

My Paese

Dream of a summer's day.

What a continuous shivery
bell-ringing of cicadas!
The prevailing north-west wind
was stirring the withered leaves:
they rasped, along their rows.

Among the elms the sun
set, in its dusty wrappings.
The sky had only two
clouds, thin, eaten away:
two white strokes of a brush

on the whole dark blue sky.

Hedges of pomegranate,
thickets of tamarisk,
the distant regular throb
of someone's threshing machine,
the silvery *angelus*...

where was I? Those bells
told me where I was,
weeping, while a dog
was barking at the outsider
who walked with his face to the ground.

GIOVANNI PASCOLI
'From Dawn to Sunset' VII, from *Myricae*

Sapienza

Sali pensoso la romita altura
ove ha il suo nido l'aquila e il torrente,
e centro della lontananza oscura
    sta, sapïente.

Oh! scruta intorno gl'ignorati abissi:
più ti va lungi l'occhio del pensiero,
più presso viene quello che tu fissi:
    ombra e mistero.

GIOVANNI PASCOLI
'Pensieri' III

Di lassù

La lodola perduta nell'aurora
si spazia, e di lassù canta alla villa,
che un fil di fumo qua e là vapora;

di lassù largamente bruni farsi
i solchi mira quella sua pupilla
lontana, e i bianchi bovi a coppie sparsi.

Qualche zolla nel campo umido e nero
luccica al sole, netta come specchio:
fa il villano mannelle in suo pensiero,
e il canto del cuculo ha nell'orecchio.

GIOVANNI PASCOLI
'L'ultima passeggiata' II

Wisdom

Climb with your thoughts up to the lonely height
where the eagle and the waterfall leave their nests,
and stand as the centre of a blur of distance,
    clutching your wisdom.

O examine round you the unvisited depths:
the farther out the eye of thought can go,
the closer comes the thing you're staring into:
    mystery, shadow.

GIOVANNI PASCOLI
'Thoughts' III, from *Myricae*

From Up There

The lark, lost in the blank of dawn somewhere,
takes a walk round, and sings down to the farm,
as a thread of smoke unravels here and there;

from so far up, its little pupil stares
at furrows growing generously brown
and the scattered dots of oxen in white pairs.

In the damp black ploughland there's an upturned clod
glinting as cleanly as a piece of mirror;
the farmer's tying sheaves in sleepy thought,
and holds the song of the cuckoo in one ear.

GIOVANNI PASCOLI
'The Last Walk' II, from *Myricae*

I pastori

Settembre, andiamo. È tempo di migrare.
Ora in terra d'Abruzzi i miei pastori
lascian gli stazzi e vanno verso il mare:
scendono all'Adriatico selvaggio
che verde è come i pascoli dei monti.

Han bevuto profondamente ai fonti
alpestri, che sapor d'acqua natìa
rimanga ne' cuori esuli a conforto,
che lungo illuda la lor sete in via.
Rinnovato hanno verga d'avellano.

E vanno pel tratturo antico al piano,
quasi per un erbal fiume silente,
su le vestigia degli antichi padri.
O voce di colui che primamente
conosce il tremolar della marina!

Ora lungh'esso il litoral cammina
la greggia. Senza mutamento è l'aria.
Il sole imbionda sì la viva lana
che quasi dalla sabbia non divaria.
Isciacquìo, calpestìo, dolci romori.

Ah perchè non son io co' miei pastori?

GABRIELE D'ANNUNZIO
(1863-1938)

The Shepherds

September – let's be off. Time to migrate.
Up there in the Abruzzi now my shepherds
are leaving the folds and moving to the sea,
climbing down to the savage Adriatic –
which is green like the pastures in the mountains.

They have drunk deeply at the Alpine fountains,
hoping to make a taste of that home water
stay in their exiled hearts to comfort them,
and on the way for miles deceive their thirst.
They've cut themselves new rods of hazelwood.

They drop to the plain by the old droving road,
as if along a silent river of grass,
treading the footprints of their ancestors.
O hear the cry of the first to recognise
the shimmering of the sea against the beach!

And now the flock is walking down a reach
of shoreline. Nothing changes in the air.
The sun is fading all that living wool
until it looks the colour of the sand.
Rinsing of water, trampling feet, sweet sounds.

Ah why am I not there among my shepherds?

GABRIELE D'ANNUNZIO

Bocca d'Arno

Bocca di donna mai mi fu di tanta
soavità nell'amorosa via
(se non la tua, se non la tua, presente)
come la bocca pallida e silente
del fiumicel che nasce in Falterona.
Qual donna s'abbandona
(se non tu, se non tu) sì dolcemente
come questa placata correntìa?
Ella non canta,
e pur fluisce quasi melodìa
all'amarezza.
    Qual sia la sua bellezza
    io non so dire,
    come colui che ode
    suoni dormendo e virtudi ignote
    entran nel suo dormire.

Le saltano all'incontro i verdi flutti,
schiumanti di baldanza,
con la grazia dei giovini animali.
In catena di putti
non mise tanta gioia Donatello,
fervendo il marmo sotto lo scalpello,
quando ornava le bianche cattedrali.
Sotto ghirlande di fiori e di frutti
svolgeasi intorno ai pergami la danza
infantile, ma non sì fiera danza
come quest'una.
    V'è creatura alcuna
    che in tanta grazia
    viva ed in sì perfetta
    gioia, se non quella lodoletta
    che in aere si spazia?

The Mouth of the Arno

The mouth of woman never was to me
so full of pleasure in the ways of love
(excepting yours, excepting yours, right now)
as the pale opening out, the silent lips
of this small stream that springs in Falterona.
What woman can abandon
herself (excepting only you) so sweetly
as this appeased and sated current does?
It does not sing
and yet it flows like melody towards
its bitter end.
  The nature of its beauty
  I cannot speak,
  being like one who hears
  sounds that pierce his sleep, and unknown powers
  enter his sleeping mind.

Leaping a little to meet it the green waves
burst into confident foam,
the graceful surging of young animals.
They move with greater bounds
of joy than Donatello's hand-in-hand
cherubs in marble warm beneath the chisel
when he was decorating white cathedrals.
Under the swags and chains of flowers and fruits
those children wreath around his balustrades,
skipping and turning; but their dance is never
as wild as this one.
  Does any other creature
  live with such grace
  and in such perfect joy? –
  except for Dante's lark up there
  that goes for walks on air.

Forse l'anima mia, quando profonda
sé nel suo canto e vede la sua gloria;
forse l'anima tua, quando profonda
sé nell'amore e perde la memoria
degli inganni fugaci in che s'illuse
ed anela con me l'alta vittoria.
Forse conosceremo noi la piena
felicità dell'onda
libera e delle forti ali dischiuse
e dell'inno selvaggio che si sfrena.
Adora e attendi!
    Adora, adora, e attendi!
    Vedi? I tuoi piedi
    nudi lascian vestigi
    di luce, ed a' tuoi occhi prodigi
    sorgon dall'acque. Vedi?

Grandi calici sorgono dall'acque,
di non so qual leggiere oro intessuti.
Le nubi i monti i boschi i lidi l'acque
trasparire per le corolle immani
vedi, lontani e vani
come in sogno paesi sconosciuti.
Farfalle d'oro come le tue mani
volando a coppia scoprono su l'acque
con meraviglia i fiori grandi e strani,
mentre tu fiuti
l'odor salino.
    Fa un suo gioco divino
    l'Ora solare,
    mutevole e gioconda
    come la gola d'una colomba
    alzata per cantare.

Perhaps my soul when it has thrown itself
deep in its state of song and sees its glory,
perhaps your soul when it has thrown itself
deep into love and so forgets the history
of the illusions it was trapped among
and strains with me toward high victory –
perhaps we shall experience the full
happiness of the free
overlapping wave, the strong unfolded wings
and the untamed expansion of its song.
Keep watch, and worship.
        Keep praying, watch with awe.
        You see? Your bare
        feet have left prints of light,
        and before your eyes wonders are rising
        out of the water. See?

Great flower-cups, chalices, rise from the pouring water,
woven somehow like mail from finest gold.
The clouds the hills the woods the shores the waters
are visible through the enormous flower-heads,
you see? – far-off, transparent
as unknown countries that appear in dreams.
Butterflies golden as your open hands
flying in pairs discover on the waters
with wonder those great blossoms that seem foreign,
while you breathe in
the smell of salt.
        The long hand of the sun
        plays its divine game
        with shifting shades of joy,
        like the iridescent throats of pigeons
        lifting, swollen with song.

Sono le reti pensili. Talune
pendon come bilance dalle antenne
cui sostengono i ponti alti e protesi
ove l'uom veglia a volgere la fune;
altre pendono a prua dei palischermi
trascorrendo il perenne
specchio che le rifrange; e quando il sole
batte a poppa i navigli, stando fermi
i remi, un gran fulgor le trasfigura:
grandi calici sorgono dall'acque,
gigli di foco.
      Fa un suo divino gioco
      la giovine Ora
      che è breve come il canto
      della colomba. Godi l'incanto,
      anima nostra, e adora!

GABRIELE D'ANNUNZIO
(1863-1938)

This vision is the fishermen's hanging nets.
Some hang like parts of balances slung from spars
propped up on the high platforms which jut out
where men can sit and watch and pull the rope;
others are hung over the bows of dories,
and cut the eternal mirror
of passing water that reflects them; when the sun
beats on the boats from astern and the oars stand
at rest, a burst of radiance transforms them:
great chalices, flower-cups, rise from the pouring waters,
lilies of fire.
      The young face of the sun
      plays its divine game,
      which lasts no longer than
      the song of pigeons. Enjoy enchantment,
      our single soul: worship here.

GABRIELE D'ANNUNZIO

Ulisse

Nella mia giovanezza ho navigato
lungo le coste dalmate. Isolotti
a fior d'onda emergevano, ove raro
un uccello sostava intento a prede,
coperti d'alghe, scivolosi, al sole
belli come smeraldi. Quando l'alta
marea e la notte li annullava, vele
sottovento sbandavano piú al largo,
per fuggirne l'insidia. Oggi il mio regno
è quella terra di nessuno. Il porto
accende ad altri i suoi lumi; me al largo
sospinge ancora il non domato spirito,
e della vita il doloroso amore.

UMBERTO SABA
(1883-1957)

Ulysses

When I was growing up, I used to sail
down the Dalmatian coast. There were low islets
barely surfacing from the waves, where sometimes
a bird or two would wait, head bent for prey:
reefs masked in seaweed, slippery, in the sunlight
pretty as emeralds. When the higher tides
or darkness cancelled them from sight, the sails
caught on a lee shore would tack out to sea,
to escape these lurking dangers. Now my kingdom
is just that land that Noman owns. The harbour
puts on its lights for others: I am driven
still towards open sea by the untamed breath
and by the aching of desire for life.

UMBERTO SABA

I fiumi

Mi tengo a quest'albero mutilato
abbandonato in questa dolina
che ha il languore
di un circo
prima o dopo lo spettacolo
e guardo
il passaggio quieto
delle nuvole sulla luna

Stamani mi sono disteso
in un'urna d'acqua
e come una reliquia
ho riposato

L'Isonzo scorrendo
mi levigava
come un suo sasso

Ho tirato su
le mie quattr'ossa
e me ne sono andato
come un acrobata
sull'acqua

Mi sono accoccolato
vicino ai miei panni
sudici di guerra
e come un beduino
mi sono chinato a ricevere
il sole

Questo è l'Isonzo
e qui meglio
mi sono riconosciuto
una docile fibra
dell'universo

Il mio supplizio
è quando
non mi credo
in armonia

The Rivers

I hold onto this badly wounded tree
abandoned in this limestone swallow-hole
which has the listless air
of a circus ring
before or after the show
and watch
the quiet parade
of clouds across the moon

This morning I stretched out
in a potful of water
and like a holy relic
lay back and rested

The Isonzo flowing by
was smoothing me off
like one of its stones

I pulled in
all of my limbs
and let myself go
like an acrobat
onto the water

I squatted down
near my clothes
soiled with war
and like a Bedouin
prostrated myself to receive
the sun

This is the Isonzo
and here I got to know
myself better
an impressionable fibre
of the universe

My torture
is when
I don't believe myself
in harmony

Ma quelle occulte
mani
che m'intridono
mi regalano
la rara
felicità

Ho ripassato
le epoche
della mia vita

Questi sono
i miei fiumi

Questo è il Serchio
al quale hanno attinto
duemil'anni forse
di gente mia campagnola
e mio padre e mia madre

Questo è il Nilo
che mi ha visto
nascere e crescere
e ardere d'inconsapevolezza
nelle estese pianure

Questa è la Senna
e in quel suo torbido
mi sono rimescolato
e mi sono conosciuto

Questi sono i miei fiumi
contati nell'Isonzo

Questa è la mia nostalgia
che in ognuno
mi traspare
ora ch'è notte
che la mia vita mi pare
una corolla
di tenebre

GIUSEPPE UNGARETTI
(1888-1970)

But those secret
hands
which pummel me like bread
present me
with a rare
happiness

I went back through
the stages
of my life

These
are my rivers

This one is the Serchio
where perhaps two millennia
of my country people
have drawn water
my father and mother too

This one is the Nile
which saw me
born and growing
and burning with ignorance
in its wide-spread plains

This one is the Seine
in whose cloudiness
I mixed myself again
and knew myself

These are my rivers
counted in the Isonzo

This is my longing for return
that in each of them
shines out to me
now that it's night –
so that my life appears to me
a flower-head
of darknesses

GIUSEPPE UNGARETTI

Mattina

M'illumino
d'immenso

GIUSEPPE UNGARETTI

Morning
(versions)

I bring myself light
out of immensity

I turn on
my own
endless free light

I light
me
from endless space

I become an illumination
of myself
with unlimited colour

I throw on me
infinite light

[We were lit by flares
all night

Now]

I display myself in light
from unmeasured

[single
continuing
natural
sun]

GIUSEPPE UNGARETTI

NOTES

The Italian texts printed here are taken from standard editions by scholarly editors. We have checked these for misprints, but have not attempted to iron out any inconsistencies. We are grateful to Arnoldo Mondadori Editore for arranging permission to print and translate the poems by Saba and Ungaretti, which are still in copyright. I am grateful to the editor of *Liquid Crystals Today*, who first published some lines from one of my Petrarch versions.

I would also like to thank a number of friends and scholars for suggestions and help. All errors however are my own.

Italian Verse

A word on Italian versification might be useful, although the Italian big verse-line is not unlike the English iambic pentameter (with a feminine ending) and this line is often stressed in a way that is not totally unrecognisable to an English ear.

The Italian "standard" line, then, is called the endecasillabo: it has eleven syllables but otherwise has nothing in common with, for example, Catullus' hendecasyllables. It can have a clear iambic rhythm: thus

> Lo maggior corno della fiamma antica   [*Inferno* XXVI, 85]

seems straightforward, if one bears in mind that a vowel at the end of a word elides (doesn't count) before an initial vowel *(fiamm' antica*, from the metrical point of view). But the lines that follow

> comminciò a crollarsi mormorando,
> pur come quella cui vento affatica.

need further explanation. The accented final vowel of *comminciò* doesn't elide – in fact, accented final vowels and accented monosyllables don't elide. And *cui* counts as a single syllable. Apart from this, the only difficulty is an unfamiliar wildness of rhythm, both lines being less monotonously accented than any English poet except Browning would go in for.

To sum up, the Italian line can occasionally seem almost as free as syllabics, till one acquires an ear for it. But the metrical principles are very simple, and poems can be in trochees, etc, as well as rhythmically fluid in the way demonstrated.

Finally, the rhymes are like English rhymes, except that they are more usually feminine than masculine (which give a ten-syllable line). I think there are no triple rhymes (*rime sdrucciole*) in this book – they have the same slightly unserious air they have in English.

These rules of thumb can be supplemented and elaborated by consulting a manual like W.T. Elwert's *Versificazione italiana dalle origini ai giorni nostri* (Firenze, Felice Le Monnier, 1973).

Comments

Psalm of the Creatures *(pages 8-11)*: According to tradition, St Francis composed this poem (or rather song) during a night of illness in 1225, and dictated it in the morning to one of his companions, in the garden of his church San Damiano in Assisi.

Formally, the poem is a psalm; that is, the lines are of various lengths but are designed to be sung to a psalm tune. In subject, it is closely related to the Benedicite and to Psalm 148, the first of the three psalms called Lauds ('Praises').

I concentrated on making my version singable and made no attempt to represent the assonantal rhymes – a phenomenon standard in Spanish poetry but seldom found in Italian poetry after the early period. The most difficult word is the recurring *per*, which has caused much controversy. A comparison with Psalm 148 ('Praise ye him, sun and moon') shows that it might mean *by*, but this will not work in line 27 ('praised *by* Death'?); it is tempting to confuse it with its modern meaning *for* ('may you be praised *for* Sister water'), but it certainly means 'through' in line 14 and I incline to think it best to use *through* each time it occurs. Thus, instead of praising God directly (which we are unworthy to do, line 4), we praise him *through* the things he has created. This interpretation is the one favoured by C. Dionisotti and C. Grayson, whose text I have used here. In their book *Early Italian Texts* (1965) they use the title 'Laudes Creaturarum'. The poem has also been called 'Canticum Fratris Solis'.

An Englishman in Hell *(pages 12-13)*: Adamo di Brescia was burned at the stake in Florence for forging Florentine coin when Dante was about sixteen. Adamo was possibly English.

Sonnet 164 *(pages 14-15)*: The bandage or blindfold of love and art almost excludes the world; but round the edge of the carefully woven cloud of feeling can be glimpsed an occasional natural object.

Shepherdesses *(pages 18-19):* This pastoral ballad has more countryside in its friendly world than other examples of the genre. In D.G. Rossetti's translation (in his *The Early Italian Poets*), the order of the first two stanzas is inexplicably reversed.

Hawking for Partridges *(pages 20-39):* This poem may serve for contrast: its fairly utilitarian attitude to landscape reveals the colouring of other poets' literary spectacles. The text is taken from Emilio Bigi's selection of Lorenzo's writings (second edition, Torino, 1965); an interestingly different version can be found in Corinna Salvadori's selection (University College Dublin, 1992). The numbers in bold below are are stanza-numbers.)

4 *(page 21):* It seemed best to translate the dogs' names literally and forget rhyme for the moment; these are possibly the names of real family dogs. The last name, Pennecchio, really refers to the handful of wool on the distaff before it's turned into yarn (on the spindle): I imagine the puppy had a fluffy tail; hence, Plume. As for Serchio, this dog seems to be named after the river where the people of Lucca used to swim (*Inferno* XXI, 49) or get their water (see Ungaretti's 'I fiumi', in this book) and where Shelley used to sail ('The Boat on the Serchio').

5 *(page 23):* 'Guglielmo' is probably Guglielmo dei Pazzi who married Lorenzo's sister Bianca. There seem to be several plays on the family name of Pazzi ('the Mad Ones'). 'Matto' (stanza 35) and 'furia', 'pazienza', and 'prudenza' (stanza 36) all seem like digs in the ribs.

10 *(page 25):* 'Our hero with The Nose' is the poet Luigi Pulci, author of *Morgante*.

13 *(page 25):* 'Il Parente' might be merely somebody's surname, but I feel it could refer to Lorenzo's father Piero (died 1469) or perhaps more likely to his grandfather Cosimo, who died in 1464, when Lorenzo was fifteen. I think the next line could only refer to someone important to the poet. 1464 would be a good narrative date for the poem as it appears to be an account of a day out when Lorenzo was too young to be one of the falconers himself, but his friend Guglielmo was just old enough.

26 *(page 31):* There's a pun here on 'spennecchia' (to pluck feathers off, and hence to fleece – as we would say), but not a particularly illuminating one, since it seems not to apply in its main plain sense. I think the 'old' bird must have been clever enough to get away, the hawk being left standing. I assume Lorenzo wants *spennecchia* to mean the falconer made a mess of it and lost face.

28 *(page 31):* The hawk is 'perfetto' – fully trained – 'made' being the English technical term. The partridge is caught in the air but then disappears (at least from the story as told). The Italian editors seem to think the passage means that the hawk has been indisciplined and bloodied its claws and beak on the prey instead of giving it up unmarked to its master, but it seems to me Lorenzo is being deliberately vague: he wants to show the puzzlement of the moment: has the hawk caught it and let it go, or eaten it very quickly, or what?

31-34 *(page 32):* The narrative here is very condensed and elliptical; I hope my version makes the right sense of it.

32 *(page 32):* Line 3 (literally 'it seems that he says something like this to Guglielmo') might be an attempt to describe the assumption of somebody observing the scene from a distance and guessing at what is said. 'In a bate' (the translator's contribution to narrative clarity here) is a falconry term, and refers to the fluttering and often upside down raging of frustrated hawks in training.

41 *(page 37):* 'trebbiano' would normally mean a variety of white wine from the Romagna, the region north of Tuscany. But *il Trebbio* is the name of one of the Medici villas (at Cafaggiolo), so perhaps Lorenzo means the family's own best wine. In fact, this estate (in the Mugello valley, about 15 miles north of Florence) would seem to be a very good candidate for the scene of the poem.

44 *(page 37):* Lorenzo seems to be alluding to the school of poets of Dante's youth, the 'dolce stil novo'.

45 *(page 39):* The caverns (or perhaps river-banks, for *grotte* has several meanings) have not been identified.

The oracular last couplet of the poem seems to refer to or to be referred to by a letter of Pulci's to Lorenzo (27 July 1473) which contains a not very clear remark about rhymes harder than '*zucchero*'. Possibly Pulci had commented adversely on Lorenzo's sometimes lazy rhymes – and his rhythms. Maybe the letter also helps date the composition of the poem, presumably written before the Conspiracy of the Pazzi (Easter 1478) – in which Guglielmo was not in fact implicated.

Orlando Furioso *(pages 46-47):* Canto X, stanza 113 has a neat pair of matching sexual landscapes.

Gerusalemme Liberata: Canto III, stanza 4 *(page 49):* Tasso is comparing the first sight of Jerusalem with the first sight of America (about fifty years before he was born). Stanza 7 *(page 51):* Apparently the detail about bare feet is historical, not a 'conceit'.

Canto XII *(pages 52/53):* Tasso wonderfully does not say so, but this classic experience (of being suckled by a tiger), so often referred to apropos of hard hearts, must be meant to explain how Clorinda grew up to be a warrior.

Canto XIV, stanza 70 *(pages 58-59):* This mountain in the sea seems to be the same montagna ('bruna / per la distanza') which Dante says Ulysses saw before his boat sank in the Atlantic (*Inferno* XXVI, 133-34). That mountain turned out to be the holy hill of Purgatorio, a good contrast to Armida's magic isle of pleasure.

Italia, Italia *(pages 62-63):* This sonnet was translated by Byron into two stanzas (18 lines) of *Childe Harold's Pilgrimage* (Canto IV, xlii-iii).

To Zante *(pages 64-65):* Zante (Zacynthus), off the west coast of the Peloponnese, is the most southerly of the Ionian Islands. When Foscolo was born it had belonged to Venice for centuries. He and his family moved to Venice when he was four, and a few years later Zante became (briefly) French. It is now part of Greece.

Belli sonnets *(pages 66-69):* I apologise for not being able to represent Belli's Roman dialect. Robert Garioch did a marvellous job on some fifty of the other 2000-odd sonnets in his *Collected Poems* (1977).

The Infinite *(pages 70-71):* The hill in 'L'infinito' is near Recanati (a hill-town near Ancona), where Leopardi was born and bred.

Flowering Broom *(pages 76-91):* 'La ginestra' has also been translated by Edwin Morgan, among others, including (with facing text and notes) G.L. Bickersteth in his *The Poems of Leopardi* (1923). A few comments may be useful here.

The optimistic words quoted ironically at the end of the first stanza are from a poem by Leopardi's cousin Terenzio Mamiani, also a poet.

'Barbarism' meant to Leopardi a bastard stage between the 'savagery' of the Golden Age and a state of true civilisation. For example, he took it that the 'Indians' of North America were destroying each other by inter-tribal fighting and drunkenness because they were beginning, imperfectly, to be civilised (so he wrote in his notebook on 7 July 1826).

Matthew Arnold quoted the fourth stanza (beginning 'Often upon these slopes') in *Essays in Criticism*, second series, to show 'the full superiority of Leopardi to Byron in philosophic thought and in the expression of it'.

Mergellina is a suburb at the north end of the Bay of Naples, with a small port from which one catches boats to Capri and Ischia.

The descriptions of eruptions in the poem derive both from the Younger Pliny (on the AD 79 eruption) and from witnesses of the 1835 one. (The poem was written in 1836 in a small villa south-east of Naples.)

St Ambrose's *(pages 92-97):* In 1796-97, in a lightning campaign, the young general Napoleon conquered Lombardy and 'liberated' the Italians. Italy was carved up into nominally free republics, and when Napoleon fell and the Austrians regained political control over northern Italy, they found this taste of freedom had made a national Italian patriotism possible. Giusti is writing just before the first peninsula-long outbreaks of revolution against foreign domination.

Giosuè Carducci *(pages 98-115):* These *Odi Barbare* are so called because although they appear to use Greek metres (Sapphics and Alcaeics, etc) and to be in the Horatian tradition, they don't use the metres correctly, as Horace did, but "barbarously" – i.e. in a non-Greek manner. Thus the Sapphic stanza (−∘−−− ∘∘− ∘−− [three times] −∘∘−−) becomes simply three eleven-syllable lines followed by a five-syllable line. The reader will see that I have made the mistake of rendering the first two of these poems "correctly", that is, by using a stressed syllable to represent a Greek "long" syllable. This was not Carducci's way, and in the Clitumnus ode I have simply (and correctly) written syllabics.

Facing the Baths of Caracalla *(pages 98-101):* The human or divine history of a view is what catches Carducci's interest – one might almost say he writes about Italian scenes like an awestruck foreigner. Here he makes the Alban ('white') Hills remind us of a mountain in Horace, Soracte, which also 'stood white with snow' (*Odes* I.9). In stanza 4 the ruined Baths are like Pelion piled on Ossa by the Giants who rebelled against Zeus. In stanza 7, Cicero is quoted to the effect that there was once on the Palatine an altar dedicated to the goddess Febris (Fever). The word Palatine comes from the home-town in the Peloponnese of the original colonist Evander, and the top of the Palatine, the early Rome of Romulus and Remus, was roughly square and was in ancient times some-times called Roma Quadrata. Saturnian was an early Italian metre that was superseded by the Greek metres that most extant Latin verse is written in. 'Saturnian' has a hint of the Golden Age too – 'our' golden age (in Italy). 'Capena' (stanza 10) seems to be short-hand for the whole Porta Capena district (near those Baths), not just the Gate. It was one of the fourteen Regiones (city wards, later called Rioni by the Italians) that Augustus divided Rome into for urban administration. Carducci probably says 'Capena' also because 'Porta Capena' might give us the unfortunate image of the body of divine Rome constricted in the gateway as by a napkin-ring. He is after the image of a huge cloudy beauty lying across the cityscape.

At the Springs of the Clitumnus *(pages 106-115):* This is in Umbria, about ten miles south of Foligno on the road to Spoleto. The place, famous since antiquity, has also been described by the Younger Pliny, Goethe (*Italian Journey*), and Byron (*Childe Harold's Pilgrimage*, Canto IV, lxvi-viii), among many others. The historical references don't really need elucidating.

Giovanni Pascoli *(pages 116-121):* I understand that Pascoli's birthplace, San Mauro di Romagna, has been renamed San Mauro Pascoli in his honour. This puts him in the rare category of people who have become a landscape, not quite the same as having a city named after you; more like Edward Thomas' characters Jenny Pinks and Old Farmer Hayward who are remembered as copses or lanes.

Ulysses *(pages 130-131):* Dante made the ageing Ulysses a seeker after more knowledge than is allowed, and therefore an 'evil counsellor' of his friends, which is why he is in the *Inferno* (Canto XXVI). Tennyson took up the story-line but made him out to be simply a restless hero, not a dangerous and evil man. Saba makes Ulysses' quest for knowledge personal and tragic again, cruising the cultural wilderness of the sea for possibly fatal experiences.

Morning *(pages 136-137):* Perhaps 'Mattina' is Ungaretti's best-known poem, partly because of its extreme brevity. It is a landscape poem with no landscape in it, no history, and no person but the narrator. Like 'I fiumi' it comes from a soldier's view of nature, being written presumably after or during a night in the open, in danger; for Ungaretti began his career as Italy's war poet of the Great War. The many possible meanings to be savoured in each word are an effect deliberately aimed at by Ungaretti, which caused him to be given the doubtless irritating label of 'hermetic'.